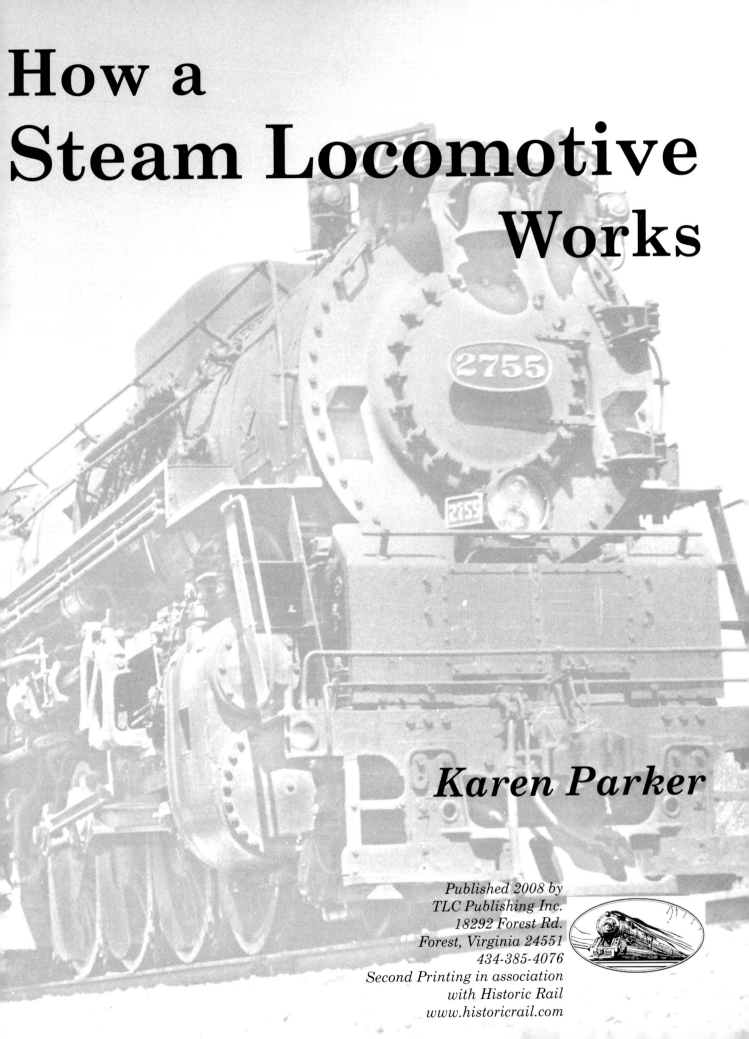

How a
Steam Locomotive
Works

Karen Parker

Published 2008 by
TLC Publishing Inc.
18292 Forest Rd.
Forest, Virginia 24551
434-385-4076
Second Printing in association
with Historic Rail
www.historicrail.com

Front Cover: C&O K-4 2-8-4 #2780, photo by Jack Manor, C&O Historical Society Collection.

Front End Sheets: This photo of a Nickel Plate 2-8-4 receiving a bath provides an excellent view of its running gear, photo by Richard Cook, Thomas W. Dixon, Jr. Collection.

Back End Sheets: This unusual overhead view of several C&O Allegheny type (2-6-6-6) locomotives provides a clear view of the top of the boiler and tender, and the appliances mounted there. C&O Railway Photo, C&O Historical Society Collection.

Back Cover: a NYC Niagara (4-8-4) at speed. Thomas W. Dixon, Jr. Collection

A note on photo and illustration credits:
Unless otherwise noted, all photos are from the collection of the C&O Historical Society (COHS).
Unless otherwise noted, all drawings and figures were made by the author.
Illustrations credited "COMLF" are from the *Manual for Locomotive Firemen* of the Chesapeake & Ohio Railway.
Illustrations credited to "Bruce" are from *The Steam Locomotive in America*, by Alfred W. Bruce.
Photos credited to "Lima" are by the Lima Locomotive Works.
Photos credited to "Baldwin" are by the Baldwin Locomotive Works.
Photos credited to "Alco" are by the American Locomotive Co.

Published by TLC Publishing
18292 Forest Rd.
Forest, Virginia 24551
434-385-4076
www.tlcrailroadbooks.com

ISBN 978-0-939-48789-9

Library of Congress Catalog Control Number 2008908580

Foreword

Bill Withuhn
Curator of Transportation History
Smithsonian Institution

The steam locomotive is fascinating, in part, because it is so simple in its basic concept – what could be simpler than boiling water, making steam, and pushing a couple of pistons? And yet it embodies an uncounted myriad of design and mechanical subtleties, all resulting from design challenges that were met during a century-and-a-half by the very best in human ingenuity.

At least six generations of talented design engineers and mechanics rose to these challenges with remarkably clever and sophisticated problem-solving. The more one studies the subject, the more amazing the design solutions become. Ponder just two indicators: in its time, the piston-powered steam locomotive went from some 4 horsepower to nearly 8,000 horsepower, and from 4 miles an hour to more than 125 miles an hour, yet fit on the same gauge track.

Karen Parker is that rare kind of writer who has an outstanding professional background in the field necessary for accurate understanding of her subject (in this case, physics and mechanical engineering), and who also has the uncommon knack of bringing her explanations down to earth for general readers. Her explanations are clear, concise, devoid of esoteric terms, and written for those who enjoy understanding mechanical things, but who are not deeply conversant with steam technology and would like to know more.

A book like this has been long overdue. Most previous book-length explanations for general readers of how a steam locomotive works have been pretty slim volumes. Such books are much too oversimplified to appeal to adults who have a hunger to know more – beyond just "boiling water, making steam, and pushing a piston."

Such readers can explore many other sources – in magazines, on the Web, in books for railfans, and in textbooks and manuals published in the first half of the 20th century for steam designers and mechanics. But what's found is either material written for practitioners of that era who were already steeped in the technology, or newer material that usually depends on background knowledge familiar to fans of steam locomotives. Such fans – and I'm certainly one – often speak in an exotic language all their own. Lacking for most modern readers are good explanations of the fundamental components of the steam locomotive, in one good source that puts the components together.

This book answers that long-standing need. Two levels of clear, succinct explanations are here for readers to explore: basic but more satisfying than are often found, and (in the optional sidebars) a bit more advanced, aimed at those who remember something of their high-school physics.

The illustrations are a major part of this book's clarity. Drawings alone can fail to show relationships among the various parts visible on real locomotives, and photographs alone often fail as well. Combined here to make a well-chosen whole are photos of actual locomotives showing various details highlighted, accompanying drawings, and succinct texts. The galleries of locomotive action shots allow the reader to see variations in practice.

The author and I both hope that readers of her book will find enough here to satisfy adult curiosity, plus a bit more. And we hope such readers – now equipped with a reliable understanding of the fundamentals – will want to delve deeper.

DT&I 2-8-4 #703 at Springfield, OH, December 26, 1938.

KCS 2-10-4 #909 at Kansas City, Mo, March 20, 1938.

GN S-2 4-8-4 #2576

Contents

Foreword 3

Introduction 7

Part 1: Making it Go–Pistons and Cylinders and Valves 9

Pistons, Cylinders, and Valves 10

Slide Valves 11

Cylinder Cocks 11

Technical Details: Tractive Effort and Piston Thrust...*12*

Valve Gear 13

Technical Details: Poppet Valves...*14*

Compounding 17

Three Cylinder Locomotives 18

Wheel Arrangements 20

Part 2: Making Steam–The Boiler, Firebox, and Superheater 25

Firebox Construction 26

Oil Burning Locomotives 29

Technical Details: Train Resistance, Tractive Effort, Horsepower and Furnace Volume..*30*

Exhaust and Drafting 32

Superheating 32

Technical Details: Superheating, Tractive Effort, Horsepower, and Efficiency *33*

Technical Details: Where Does the Energy Go?..*34*

Part 3: The Foundation–Frame, Drivers, and Other Wheels.............................39

The Frame..39

Driving Wheels and Rods...41

Crossheads and Crosshead Guides 43

Technical Details: Counterbalancing *44*

Springing and Equalization..45

Lead and Trailing Trucks 45

Pilots 48

Part 4: Auxiliaries–Stoker, Feedwater, Air Pumps, etc. 55

Stokers 55

Smoke Consumers 56

Injectors 57

Feedwater Heaters 57

Low Water Alarm 59

Technical Details: the Bernoulli Effect and Its Application to Locomotive Appliances *59*

Blow Down 60

Sanding 60

Booster 61

Air Brakes..62

Lubrication 63

Generator, Headlight, Whistle and Bell 63

Smoke Deflectors 64

Builder's Plates...64

Part 5: Cab and Controls 69

The Cab..69

Contents (continued)

Cab Interior and Controls 70

The Steam Turret 72

Part 6: The Tender **73**

Part 7: "Different" Locomotives **79**

Streamlined Locomotives 79

Cab Forward Locomotives 79

Duplex Drive Locomotives 80

Water Tube Boilers and High Pressure 81

Camelbacks 82

Geared Locomotives 83

Fireless Locomotives 84

Afterword **95**

Acknowledgments and References **95**

C&O Railway Photo, COHS Collection

Doing what it was built to do, C&O K-4 2-8-4 #2716, older sister of our example locomotive, hauls a coal drag north near Prestonsburg, Kentucky in 1950.

Introduction

In this book I attempt to explain how a modern steam locomotive works, including all of its major sub-systems and appliances. While the emphasis will be on "modern" "Super Power" locomotives as built in the late 1930s and 1940s, I will also comment on older designs, particularly where those older locomotives have a different external appearance.

My primary goal is to enable the reader to understand in a general way how a reciprocating steam locomotive works, and to be able to recognize and understand what (almost) all of the various parts are and what their functions are. I will also explain some of the science and engineering behind the functioning and design of the locomotive, but these parts of the narrative will be clearly delineated, so if you're not interested in these more technical aspects you will be able to skip them with no real loss of your basic understanding.

In writing a book such as this, I could use a large variety of locomotives as examples, but in this case I chose not to. Rather I'll be using members of a family of locomotives that are closely related in design, specifically those developed by the Advisory Mechanical Committee of the Van Sweringen family of railroads. This has the advantage of a consistent design philosophy in my examples, and at the same time many of these locomotives are familiar fan trip and excursion locomotives, including C&O 614 and 2716, NKP 759 and 765, and Pere Marquette 1225.

As my main exemplar I'll use the C&O K-4 class 2-8-4, and in many cases locomotive number 2744 of that class, built by the Lima Locomotive Works in 1945.

Builders photo and railroad diagram sheet for C&O K-4 2-8-4 #2744.

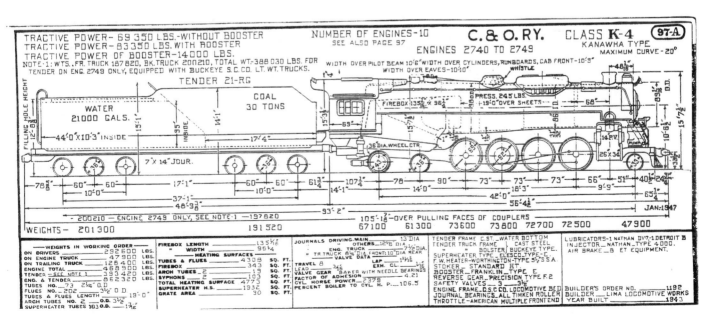

C&O K-4 2-8-4 #2747 at speed on the Big Sandy Bridge between Kentucky and West Virginia.

Part 1: Making it Go–Pistons and Cylinders and Valves

Lets begin by looking at how the energy of the steam is transformed into motion along the track – the engine part of a steam locomotive.

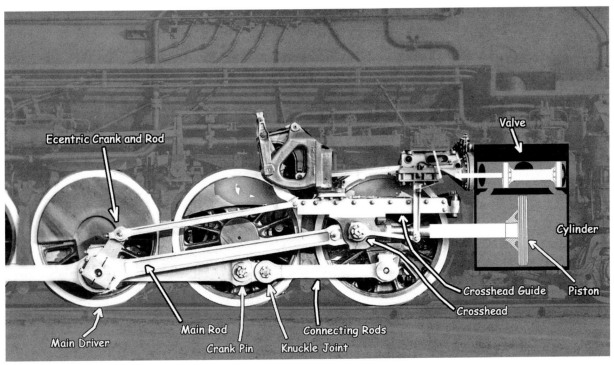

This illustration shows the major components: the *piston*, which is moved by steam pressure back and forth inside the *cylinder*, moving the *main rod* to turn the main driving wheel (or driver) via its *crank*. The other driving wheels are connected to and turned by the *connecting rods*. This is all very similar to an internal combustion engine except that steam is sequentially admitted to both sides of the cylinder and thus the piston is pushed in both directions.

Note that (for 2 cylinder locomotives) the cranks on a pair of drivers are aligned ¼ turn apart, ensuring that the four power impulses are evenly distributed, one for each ¼ turn as the wheels rotate. This also ensures that if the engine should stop with the crank at the extreme of its travel, where it can exert no thrust, the crank on the other side will be positioned where it will exert maximum thrust.

The *valve gear* takes motion from the *eccentric crank* and converts it into oscillating motion that will work the valve to admit steam into each end of the cylinders at the proper times. To do this the eccentric crank is about ¼ turn out of phase with the main crank. Note that while steam is being admitted into one end of the cylinder the other end is exhausting used steam through the exhaust ports and out the stack.

Pistons, Cylinders, and Valves

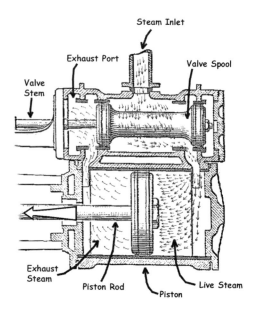

Steam Inlet

Exhaust Port

Valve Spool

Valve Stem

Exhaust Steam

Piston Rod

Piston

Live Steam

Above the cylinder and piston is the spool shaped *piston valve* which controls the admission of live steam into the cylinder and the exhaust of spent steam from the cylinder.

In operation, with the driving wheel crank fully to the bottom, the piston is centered in the cylinder and moving at its maximum speed. The valve spool is positioned all the way to the front, almost at rest, admitting steam from the boiler to the front side of the piston, and allowing any steam in the cylinder behind the piston to pass through the rear valve port into the exhaust passage. The steam flow from the boiler exerts pressure on the piston, forcing it backward, thus moving the locomotive forward.

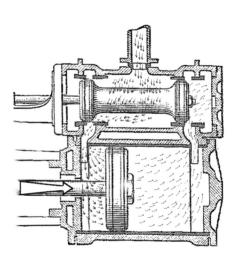

After the locomotive has moved a short distance (less than half a revolution of the drivers) the valve spool begins to move backward some, closing the steam admission port. Now the amount of steam in the cylinder in front of the piston is fixed and begins expanding, continuing to exert force on the piston but dropping in pressure and temperature. The point where this happens is called "cut off", and the locomotive engineer can control where in the piston stroke this occurs, from about 85% of the piston stroke all the way down to 20% of the piston stroke.

By the time the piston reaches the back of the cylinder the valve is moving at its maximum speed through the center of its travel, effecting a quick change over from admission at the front end of the cylinder to exhaust, and vice versa at the rear of the cylinder, reversing the direction of the piston's motion and beginning another power stroke, this time toward the front.

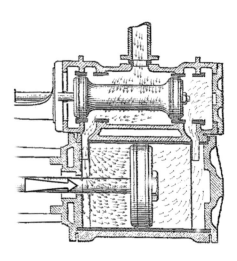

At about the point where the drivers have turned a half revolution, the valve spool has moved fully to the other end of the valve cylinder, admitting steam to the back side of the piston and fully opening the area in front of the piston to the exhaust ports. As the engine continues to roll forward, the valve again closes off the steam admission, allowing the steam in the cylinder to expand until the driver has rolled one complete turn and the cycle begins again.

Slide Valves

Early steam locomotives used slide valves rather than the piston valves described previously. In the slide valve, the steam is directed into and out of the cylinder by a block of metal that slides back and forth on a flat surface in the box-like steam chest. Slide valves fell out of favor beginning around 1910, with the advent of superheating, because the hotter superheated steam and higher boiler pressures then coming into use made it difficult to adequately lubricate the slide valves.

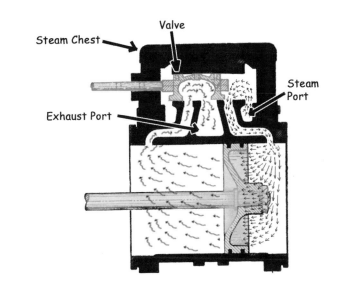

Slide valves are most commonly associated with the use of Stephenson valve gear, but this was not an exclusive relationship. Stephenson valve gear was used with piston valves, and slide valves were used with Walschaerts and Baker valve gears.

Cylinder Cocks

When a steam locomotive has been sitting for a while, the cylinders cool off and any steam present condenses to water. This water must be removed because it could damage the piston and cylinder during the exhaust stroke after the valve closes, since water in not compressible. To avoid this, locomotives are provided with *cylinder cocks*, small valves, controlled by the engineer, that vent the cylinders to the atmosphere and allow the accumulated water to be blown out. While they aren't normally visible, they are very evident when in operation, as can be seen in this photo showing the steam and water being blown out of the cylinders as the locomotive is starting.

Author Photo

11

Technical Details: Tractive Effort and Piston Thrust

The actual transmission of the force of the steam on the piston to the rim of the driving wheel is complicated by two factors

- *the steam pressure in the cylinder varies as the piston moves down the cylinder due to the cut off of steam flow from the boiler and the subsequent expansion of the steam in the cylinder,*

- *the fraction of the force on the piston rod that is translated to the driver rim is always less than 100% and in fact varies as the wheel rotates because of the geometry of the piston rod-main rod-driver crank-driving wheel linkage.*

When steam is first admitted to the cylinder, the force of the steam flow provides the force on the piston. The pressure in the cylinder is close to the boiler pressure, about 85% to 90% of boiler pressure, if the steam passages from the boiler to the cylinder are well designed. If they are not, the pressure will be less. Once the steam admission is cut off, the steam in the cylinder begins expanding and the pressure falls as the piston moves and the volume of the space containing the steam increases. This pressure drop is due to both the greater volume containing the steam and the work done by the steam in moving the piston. Chart 1 shows a typical pressure curve for 40% cut off and a boiler pressure of 245 psi, giving a cylinder chest pressure of 220 psi. As you can see the pressure in the cylinder drops from 220 psi to about 40 psi as the piston moves to the end of its stroke.

Because the crank length, which is equal to half the piston stoke, is less than the radius of the driving wheel, the force at the rim of the driver is less than the force at the crank, and in fact the ratio of the force at the rim to the force on the piston is the same as the ratio of the piston stroke to the driver diameter. For our C&O K-4, with its 34 inch stroke and 69 inch drivers, this ratio is 34/69, or 49%. In addition, the fraction of the force transmitted varies as the drivers rotate and the angle of the main rod varies with respect to the horizontal, with the maximum transmission when the wheel crank is directly above or below the wheel axle and with no force transmitted when the crank is directly in front of or behind the axle. Chart 2 shows in detail the fraction of the piston force that is transmitted to the driver rim as a function of the driver position.

If the locomotive should happen to stop with the crank positioned so that the main rod is perfectly horizontal, it couldn't get started again because none of the piston's force could be transferred to the wheel. The driving wheels on the two sides of the locomotive were always aligned so that the cranks were 90° apart, or quartered, so that if one side was on a dead spot, the other side was able to get the locomotive rolling. (Except for most three cylinder locomotives, where the cranks are separated by 120° rather than 90°.) This arrangement also has the advantage of giving the most even distribution of tractive force as the drivers rotate.

When you combine the effect of steam expansion after cut off with the effect of the varying main rod angle, and take into account the fact there are two power strokes on each side of the locomotive, the tractive force at the wheel rims varies in 4 fairly sharp pulses per driver revolution, as shown in Chart 3.

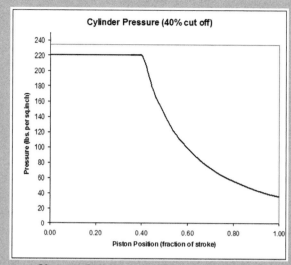

Chart 1: Cylinder pressure vs. Piston Position at 40% cut off.

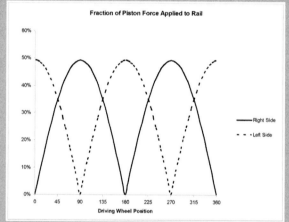

Chart 2: Percentage of the piston force applied to the driver rims for both sides vs. driver position.

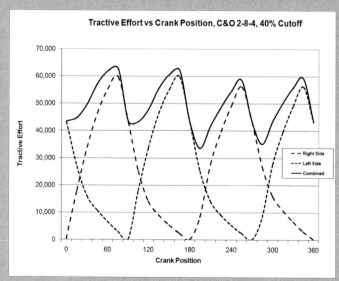

Chart 3: Tractive Effort at the driving wheel rim vs. driver position. (courtesy of Dave Stephenson)

Valve Gear

As you can see from the preceding description of how the steam is admitted to the cylinders, the proper operation of the valve is very important. The motion and control of the valve is provided by the valve gear. Over the history of steam locomotives in the United States, there have been three types of valve gear that have predominated in use: the Stephenson, the Walschaerts, and the Baker.

Stephenson Valve Gear. In this valve gear, the motion to drive the valve is taken from cams that are mounted on one of the driver axles. The only part of the valve gear that is externally visible is the rocker shaft and valve rod that transmit the valve gear motion from the valve gear between the drivers to the valves above the cylinders. Note that this valve gear is most often seen with slide valves rather than the piston valve described previously. The slide valve is a metal block that oscillates within a rectangular steam chest rather than the valve spool within a cylindrical valve chamber as previously described.

Walschaerts Valve Gear. In this valve gear the oscillating motion to drive the valve is generated by an eccentric crank mounted to the driver crank pin, oriented so that the motion is 90 degrees out of phase from the driver rotation. This oscillating motion is transferred to the link, causing it to rock back and forth. The link's rocking motion is in turn passed to the radius bar, whose end slides up and down in the slot in the link. Moving the radius bar up and down in the slot causes the

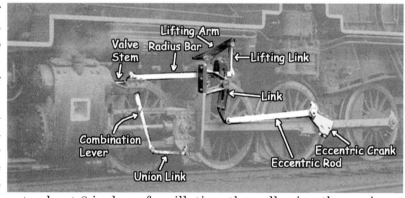

amount of motion to vary from essentially none to about 8 inches of oscillation, thus allowing the engineer to vary the cut off. The radius bar is moved up and down in the slot by the lifting arm, lifting link, and reach rod, which is controlled by the engineer.

Baker Valve Gear. In concept this gear is very similar to the Walschaerts, with the eccentric crank generating the oscillating motion that is used to drive the valve. The difference is that instead of the slotted link, the Baker gear uses a bell crank suspended from the reverse yoke to control the amount of valve motion. This has the advantage once it is set up properly, all the wear is in the pivots and bushings, which are easy to to maintain and renew.

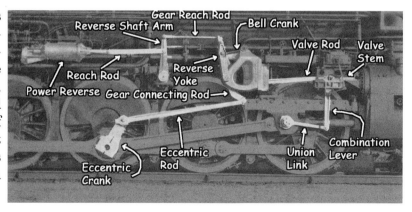

Note that with both the Walschaerts and Baker valve gears, the valve gear parts are so heavy that it is difficult for a person to move them with muscle power alone, and a power reverse was almost always used to control the valve gear. This is an air operated device that moves the valve gear parts, and is controlled by either a small lever or a control wheel in the cab. On locomotives that are not equipped with a power reverse, the reversing lever, known as the Johnson Bar, is equipped with a heavy spring to counterbalance the weight of the valve gear parts.

In the late 1930s, Franklin Railway Supply Co., a subsidiary of the Lima Locomotive Works, began development of a new type of valve and valve motion for steam locomotives. Franklin's poppet valve division was formed in 1937 to develop and commercialize the European Dabag poppet valve system, and upgrade it to make it more suitable for use on American locomotives. Franklin's first version of the poppet valve was the Type A, which used oscillating cams to drive the valves. Later, they developed the Type B, which used a rotating cam to drive the valves. Ultimately, these poppet valves were applied to 50 Pennsylvania Railroad T1 high speed passenger locomotives, 10 C&O Hudson locomotives in two different classes, one class with Type A and the other with Type B, and on a number of other locomotives on other railroads.

In order to understand the motivation for the use of poppet valves, we first need to take a look at the operation of piston valves at high speeds. The point where the moving valve closes off admission of steam into the cylinder is called "cut off", and when it occurs with respect to the position of the piston is adjustable by the engineer. When starting, the engineer will typically use a long cut off, allowing steam to be admitted into the cylinder for as much as 80% of the piston stroke. As the speed is increased, the engineer shortens the cut off, admitting steam during less and less of the piston stroke until at high speeds steam is only admitted during perhaps 20% of the piston stroke. This is done to conserve steam, since the boiler cannot supply enough steam to operate the locomotive at full cut off at high speeds.

The dashed curve in Figure 1 (right) shows the amount the valve is open both for steam admission and exhaust as the driving wheels turn through slightly more than one revolution. Here, crank angle rather than piston stroke is shown, where 0 degrees is when the crank pin is closest to the cylinder, straight ahead of the driver axle. As the cutoff is shortened, both the valve area and the duration of the valve opening become less, so that at high speeds, where very short cutoff is used, both the admission and the exhaust are very restricted. This restriction on the admission is desirable, since it causes less steam to be used, and allows the steam more time to expand, but restriction on the exhaust is highly undesirable. When the exhaust is restricted, some of the steam is left in the cylinder and compressed as the piston makes its return stroke, and this compression requires energy that would otherwise be applied to the rails as tractive effort. As the locomotive speed increases, this effect becomes more and more pronounced, resulting in a marked decline in horsepower, as shown in the dashed curve on Figure 2.

The poppet valve essentially eliminates this problem by opening and closing very rapidly, providing very high valve area regardless of cutoff, and making the operation of the exhaust valve independent of the intake valve, allowing it to remain open during most of the power stroke, significantly lowering the back pressure. In operation, the poppet valve is similar to the valves in an internal combustion engine, although they are constructed differently.

The solid curve on Figure 1 shows the valve area for the poppet valve compared to piston valves. Note that the valve opening area is greater with the poppet valves, and that the exhaust port for the poppet valve is open longer than for the piston valve. The solid curve on Figure 2 shows the effect of these changes on the horsepower vs. speed curve for a poppet valve locomotive. Note that there is essentially no fall off of power as the speed increases, indicating that the poppet valve is doing its job effectively. Note

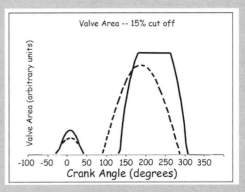

Figure 1: Valve Opening Area vs. Crank Angle

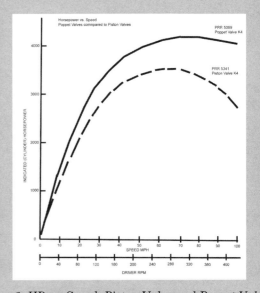

Figure 2: HP vs. Speed, Piston Valve and Poppet Valve Locomotives

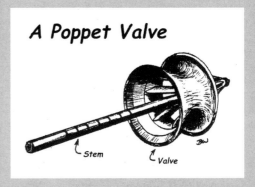

Figure 3: A typical poppet valve

too that the use of poppet valves may allow the railroad to use a less powerful locomotive in a given service than would otherwise be required with a piston valve locomotive, if the intended running speed falls within the range where poppet valves give significantly more power than piston valves.

Franklin Type A Poppet Valves

In construction, the poppet valve has dual seats and is hollow, so that when it is open, steam can flow through the valve as well as around it, as shown in Figures 3 and 5. The valves are arranged horizontally above the cylinder, in 2 sets, one for each end of the cylinder. Type A poppet valves, as were installed on the C&O L-1 Hudsons and the PRR T1 Duplexes, had 2 inlet valves above 2 exhaust valves on each end, for a total of 8 valves per cylinder, as shown in figures 4 and 5.

The Type A poppet valve system has 4 valves at each end of cylinder, driven by cams that oscillate (rock back and forth) in a cam box above the cylinder and between the valve chests, and a valve gear box on the frame along the center line of the locomotive, usually located in front of the cylinder saddle. The valve gear box contains 4 miniature Walschaerts valve gears, one each for the intake and exhaust valves for each side. Cutoff is controlled in the usual manner, with a miniature lifting link that moves the radius bar up and down in the expansion link, all done with a miniature power reverse. The oscillating motion driving the valve gear box is derived from links on the cross heads on each side of the locomotive.

Franklin Type B Poppet Valves

As noted above, after developing the Type A poppet valve, with its rather complicated drive system located on the locomotive center line, Franklin developed the Type B system, which used rotating cams to actuate the valves and a simple gear drive from the drivers to rotate the cams.

As shown in Figure 7, the Type B poppet valve has 3 valves at each end of cylinder, driven by a rotating cam in the cam box between the valve chests. The cam has three separate sections, one for each of the three valves on each end of the cylinder (the same section controls the valves at both ends of the cylinder.) The cam profile in each section varies over the length of the section, and cutoff is controlled by moving the cam transversely. The cam is driven from a crank on the main driver, coupled to the cam box by a long drive shaft with universal joints.

On the C&O, three of the Type B equipped L-2a class 4-6-4s gave excellent performance, but the other two initially gave the poppet valves a bad reputation, constantly giving trouble and frequently breaking the valve gear. During their first 50,000 mile shopping, the source of the problem was found to be the three driver sets being ¼ inch out of quarter, making it impossible to properly adjust the valve timing on the two sides of the locomotive. Once this problem was corrected, these two locomotives then gave service equivalent to their three sisters.

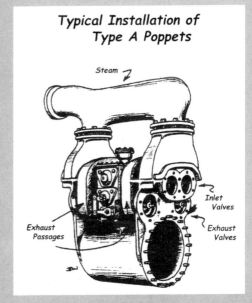

Figure 4: Typical Installation of Type A Poppet Valves

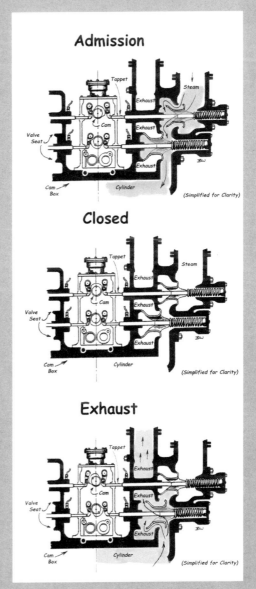

Figure 5: Type A Poppet Valve Events

15

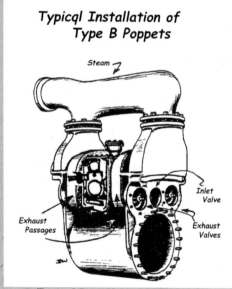

Figure 6: General Arrangement of Type A Poppet Valve Components

Type A Poppet Valve Components

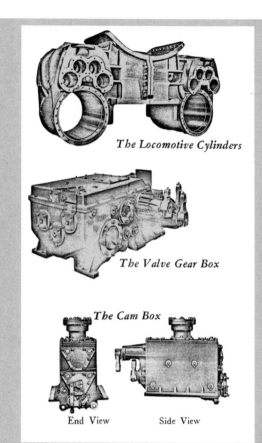

The Locomotive Cylinders

The Valve Gear Box

The Cam Box

End View   Side View

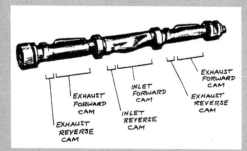

Figure 7: Typical Installation of Type B Poppet Valves

Type A Poppet Valves on a C&O L-1 Hudson

Type B Poppet Valves on a C&O L-2a Hudson

Figure 8: Rotary cam used with Type B Poppet Valves

This discussion of poppet valves is adapted from a series of articles by Bill Withuhn, published in "The Railway Enthusiasts Bulletin" in 1975 and 1976. Figures 3, 4, 6 and 8 are taken from those articles and are copyright by Bill Withuhn. Figure 7 was adapted by the author from Figure 4. Figure 5 was adapted by the author from similar figures in Bill's original article.

Compounding

In an effort to gain additional efficiency, many railroads and locomotive designers tried the concept of compounding, meaning using the exhaust steam from one set of cylinders to drive an additional set of cylinders, thereby making use of the residual heat energy in the steam after it has been used once. In North America, a variety of compound designs were tried, but only one really endured – the Mallet (pronounced "Mal-ay", the French pronunciation of the Swiss inventor's name). In the Mallet, two complete sets of cylinders and driving wheels are placed under one boiler, in two separate frames. The front engine is allowed to pivot under the boiler, allowing the locomotive to more easily negotiate curves. The front engine uses the exhaust steam from the rear engine. To allow for the fact that the pressure of the exhaust steam is much lower the cylinder diameter of the front engine is significantly larger than on the rear, high pressure, engine. In some cases, the low pressure cylinders were as large as 48" (4 feet!) in diameter. Many Mallets used slide valves on the front engine, but more modern Mallets used piston valves.

Mallet locomotives were used on many railroads, and in many cases survived right up till the last days of steam in the early 1950s, despite the basic design's origins in the first decade of the 20th century.

Note too that while all Mallets were articulated (two separate engines, hinged together, under one boiler) not all articulated locomotives were Mallets. Beginning in the 1920s, railroads began to buy "simple" articulated locomotives, with all four cylinders the same size, as a way of getting a more powerful locomotive that could still negotiate curves. The way to tell the difference is to look at the cylinders – if the front cylinders are significantly bigger than the back cylinders, the locomotive is a Mallet. If the front and back cylinders are the same size, the locomotive is a simple articulated.

A Mallet compound 2-8-8-2 locomotive of the Virginian Railroad, showing the characteristic very large low pressure cylinders on the front engine.

C&O H-8 simple articulated. Note that the cylinders on the front and rear engine are of the same size, characteristic of a simple articulated.

Three Cylinder Locomotives

In an attempt to extract more tractive effort from a locomotive, some railroads and locomotive builders developed the three cylinder locomotive. These locomotives placed the third cylinder along the locomotive centerline, between the two "normal" cylinders, with its valve next to it. The center cylinder typically would drive the second driving axle, while the outside cylinders drove the third axle. A slight bend was built into the axle for the first pair of drivers to provide clearance for the center cylinder's main rod. Rather than being quartered at 90° like a conventional locomotive, the crank pins on these machines were set 120° apart. Valve motion for the center cylinder was usually derived from the motion of the two outside valves using a "Gresley Valve Gear" with used a set of levers connected to extended valve steams projecting through the fronts of the valve chests, although a few locomotives used a third set of valve gear on the right side of the locomotive to drive the extra valve.

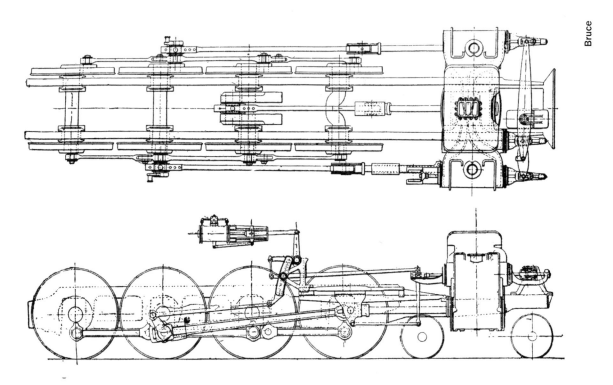

Bruce

General arrangement for a three cylinder locomotive.

18

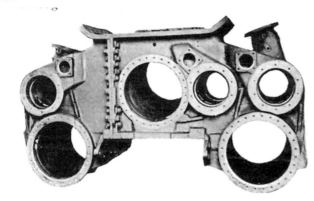

Above: a cylinder casting for a three cylinder loco-motive, viewed from the rear. The third cylinder is at the center of the casting, with its valve chamber to the right.

Below: a close-up view of the Gresley valve gear used to operate the valve for the center cylinder. The levers derive the motion for the center valve from the motion of the outside valves, connecting to the ex-tended valve stems on the front of the valve on either side.

Above: The front of a three cylinder locomotive, showing the third cylinder and its valve and the Gresley Valve Gear used to provide the proper mo-tion for the center valve.

Three cylinder locomotives tended to be big, with most having been of the 4-8-2, 4-10-2, and 4-12-2 wheel arrangement, and with one exception were all simple rather than compound. The three cylinder layout was never applied to an articulated locomotive.

Wheel Arrangements

Let's digress for a few moments to talk about the wheel arrangements used on locomotives, their names, and what kind of service each was used for. Different wheel arrangements were used on locomotives intended for different types of service, and the wheel arrangements used for each kind of service evolved over time.

Locomotive wheel arrangements are identified by a sequence of numbers denoting the number of wheels in the leading truck, the number of driving wheels, and the number of wheels in the trailing truck; for articulated locomotives like Mallet compounds or simple articulateds, a second number is used for the second set of driving wheels, resulting in a wheel arrangement consisting of four digits rather than the usual three (in Europe they count axles rather than wheels, so for instance, a locomotive that is called a 2-8-2 in North America is called a 1-4-1 in Europe.) Most wheel arrangements also have names, which were frequently references in some way or another to the railroad which first used a particular wheel arrangement. While in most cases these names were in common usage, individual railroads sometimes used their own names for certain locomotives, notably 4-8-4s, which seemed to acquire a new name on each railroad that operated it.

This table shows the wheel arrangements that were typically built new for various types of service in various time periods, along with their most common names:

Service	1880 to 1905	1905 to 1930	1930 to 1950
Switching	0-4-0 0-6-0	0-6-0 0-8-0 0-10-0	0-8-0
Mainline Passenger	4-4-0 (American or American Standard) 4-6-0 (Ten Wheel or Ten Wheeler)	4-4-2 (Atlantic) 4-6-2 (Pacific) 4-8-2 (Mountain)	4-6-4 (Hudson) 4-8-4 (Northern most commonly, but many other names)
Mainline Freight	4-4-0 (American or American Standard) 4-6-0 (Ten Wheel or Ten Wheeler) 2-8-0 (Consolidation)	2-8-2 (Mikado) 4-8-2 (Mountain)	2-8-4 (Berkshire) 2-10-4 (Texas) 4-8-4 (Northern) 4-6-6-4 (Challenger)
Heavy Freight	2-8-0 (Consolidation) 2-10-0 (Decapod)	2-8-2 (Mikado) 2-10-2 (Santa Fe) 2-6-6-2 2-8-8-2 2-10-10-2	2-10-4 (Texas) 2-6-6-6 (Allegheny) 4-6-6-4 (Challenger) 4-8-8-4 (Big boy)

Nickel Plate Mikado (2-8-2) #643 at Warrenton, Ohio.

Right: Western Pacific 4-8-4 #484 at Salt Lake City, UT in July, 1946.

Lower Right: Central of Georgia 4-8-4 #453 with Train 9, The Seminole, *near Wegrus, Ala, in August, 1948. This 4-8-4 is a close relative to the Western Pacific engine, both having been built to Southern Pacific plans during WW II.*

Bottom: Union Pacific "Big Boy" simple articulated 4-8-8-4 #4014 at Hermosa, Wy., in June, 1958. Note the double exhaust stack on this engine, one for each engine, characteristic of a simple articulated.

photo by R.H. Kennedy, Big Four Graphics collection

collection of Harold K. Vollrath

photo by R.D. Sharpless, Big Four Graphics collection

photo by Phillip H. Leroy, Big Four Graphics collection

Above: Texas &Pacific class I-1b 2-10-4 #628 and oil train at W. Weatherford, Texas in February, 1948.

Below: Boston &Albany (New York Central) class J-2 4-6-4 #617.

Big Four Graphics collection

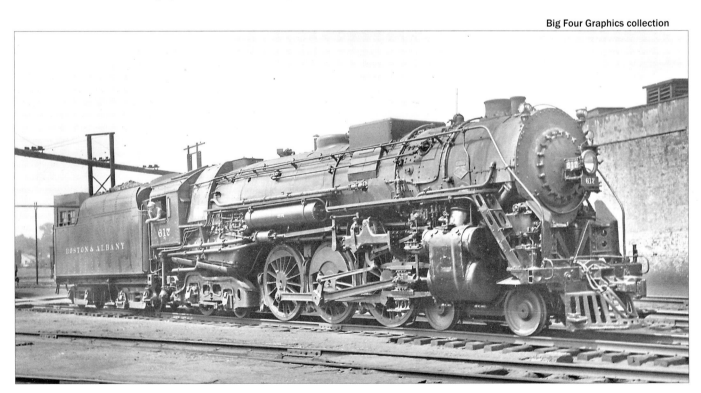

Part 2: Making Steam–The Boiler, Firebox, and Superheater

If the cylinders, pistons, and rods are the muscles of the steam locomotive, the boiler is surely its heart. Without the boiler, there would be no steam in the steam locomotive.

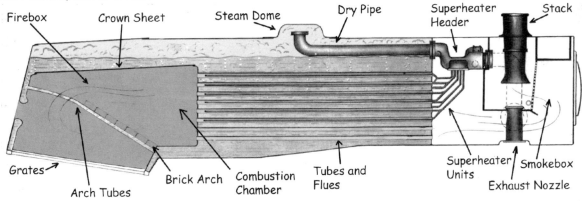

The boiler consists of a long cylindrical container made of heavy steel plate, in many cases an inch and a quarter thick, and in some large articulated locomotives up to two inches thick. At the back of the boiler is the firebox, where the fuel, either coal or oil in a modern steam locomotive, is burned to generate heat needed to boil the water. Note that the firebox is completely surrounded by water, and that it contains arch tubes which carry water through it and which support a brick arch. In front of the firebox is the combustion chamber, which allows more complete combustion of the fuel before it enters the tubes (smaller in diameter) and flues (bigger in diameter) which lead to the front of the boiler. At the bottom of the firebox is the grate which actually supports the fire as it burns.

Steam is collected from the dome which is positioned at the highest point on the boiler and flows through the dry pipe to the superheater header and throttle which are located in the smokebox, ahead of the front tube sheet, which also contains the exhaust nozzle and stack.

One very important feature of every steam locomotive boiler is the safety valves, sometimes known as "pop valves." These are set to open whenever the boiler pressure exceeds the rated boiler pressure, releasing steam and bringing the pressure down. On modern locomotives there are usually three, and sometimes four safety valves, set to open at varying pressures. For example, the four shown here on a C&O 2-6-6-6 with a rated boiler pressure of 260 psi would open at 260, 262, 264 and 266 psi respectively. These valve must be of a size and number such that they can release all the steam produced by the boiler at its maximum output.

This photo shows the boiler with most of its insulation, also known as "lagging". This magnesia and asbestos insulation was applied to the boiler to help keep the heat in, and then covered with a boiler jacket of thin steel to hold it in place and protect it from the weather.

Like virtually all modern steam locomotives, the firebox for our K-4 is entirely behind the driving wheels, with the grate below the tops of the drivers. Earlier designs had the firebox totally above the drivers, or in even earlier types, between the drivers. In a few cases modern designs were forced to put the firebox above the drivers in order to meet length constraints. Typically, engines like this were large Super Power simple articulateds such as 2-8-8-4s, 4-6-6-4s, and 4-8-8-4s, but not all super-power articulateds had fireboxes of this type. In particular, both the C&O H-8 2-6-6-6 and the N&W class A 2-6-6-4 were notable for having very large fireboxes that were located completely behind and below the tops of the driving wheels.

Firebox Construction

This photo shows a model of the firebox of a Pere Marquette 2-8-4, a sister to our C&O 2-8-4. In it you can see how the firebox is suspended inside the boiler shell by stay bolts. You can also see the mud ring, the bottom of the space between the firebox and the boiler shell. This particular firebox uses thermic syphons rather than arch tubes to allow water to circulate from the bottom of the boiler to the top through the firebox, making for a much more efficient boiler by increasing the direct heating surface.

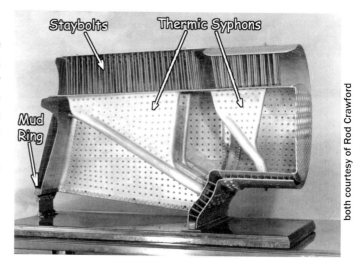

both courtesy of Rod Crawford

In this view of the model, you can see how the syphons support the brick arch. The purpose of the brick arch is to prevent the fine particles of burning coal to move directly into the tubes and flues. Forcing the burning coal to take a longer path helps to ensure that the fuel burns completely before it enters the tubes and flues, where the temperature is not high enough to support further combustion.

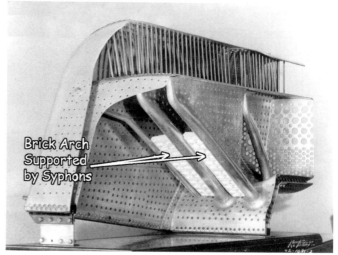

At the lower left we see the interior of the firebox of PM 2-8-4 #1225, which shows very clearly the thermic syphons. including a couple of double necked syphons, as well as giving a sense of the size of the firebox compared to the man welding one of the syphons.

The photo to the right shows of the firebox of a C&O L-2 Hudson, whose boiler and firebox are almost identical to those of the K-4 2-8-4 (called a Kanawha on the C&O, rather than the much more common name "Berkshire".) The mud ring is clearly visible, as are the two syphons, and the many staybolt holes in the crown sheet, the top of the firebox.

Locomotive Firebox Company

This cut-away drawing of a Texas & Pacific 2-10-4 illustrates how Thermic Syphons allow boiler water to circulate through the firebox.

As an alternative to thermic syphons, many locomotives had Security circulators, as seen here. Their function was the same, to allow boiler water to circulate from the cold parts of the boiler to the hotter parts, but the construction was different, making them easier to clean than syphons.

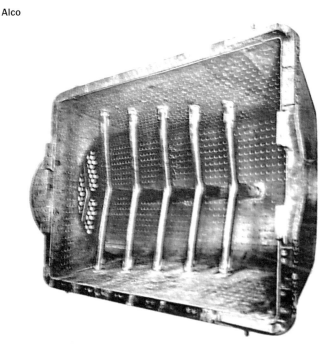

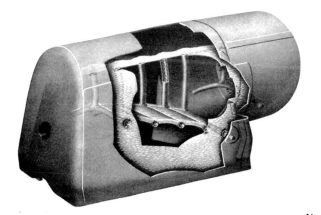

Here we see the boiler shell before the firebox is inserted. Note in particular the many many holes for the staybolts that will suspend the firebox inside the boiler shell.

This photo shows the boiler with the firebox inserted and the staybolts in place.

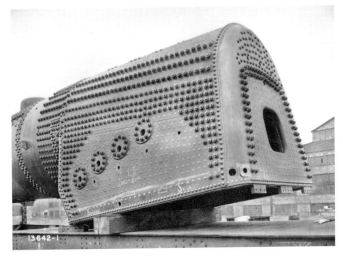

An alternative to the conventional round top boiler was the Belpaire boiler. This boiler's firebox has nearly vertical straight sides and a basically horizontal top, with a square corner where the side and top meet. Boilers of this type are most commonly associated with locomotives of the Pennsylvania and Great Northern railroads, although many roads had at least a few locomotives with this type of boiler.

This design allows a somewhat larger furnace volume and direct heating surface as compared to the more simply constructed conventional firebox, at the expense of somewhat higher construction and maintenance cost.

Bruce

As can be seen in this cross sectional view, another advantage of the Belpaire construction is that the staybolts are all very close to perpendicular to the firebox sides and top, and the top staybolts or crownstays in particular are all about the same length. These features are believed to lead to a stronger firebox and boiler.

The bottom of the firebox consists of a number of grates which support the fire, allow combustion air to enter the firebed from below, and can be moved to allow the dumping of ash. Our exemplar K-4 has 6 grates, as shown in this illustration.

The levers at the left of the illustration are the grate shaker bars. These are positioned in the cab and allow the engine crew to "shake the grates" to dump ash.

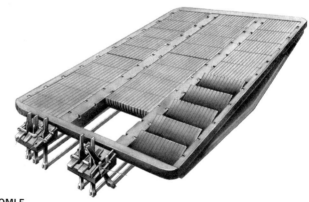

COMLF

Below the grates is an ash pan, where the ashes from the fire accumulate until they can be dumped. Ashpans can have one, two, or three hoppers, although the one on our C&O K-4 has one hopper.

As the locomotive runs, ashes accumulate in the ashpan, and ashpan capacity is one of the constraints on the range of the locomotive before it must be taken off its train and serviced, which includes dumping the ashpan into the engine terminal's ashpit.

COMLF

Note that the ashpan hopper is located between the two axles of the trailing truck, and that there is a small gap between the top of the ashpan and the bottom of the firebox sides – this gap allows combustion air to enter the firebox from below the grates.

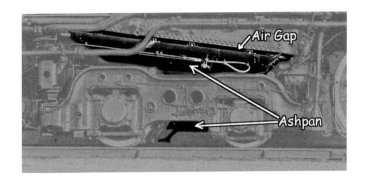

Oil Burning Locomotives

Rather than burning coal, some railroads chose to use oil to fuel some or all of their locomotives.

In an oil burning locomotive the ash pan is replaced by a nearly flat firepan, the lower part of the firebox is lined with firebrick, and an oil burner is placed at the front of the firebox, aimed toward the rear of the locomotive. Oil in the tender is heated and then piped to the oil burner, where it is atomized by the burner's steam jet and burned.

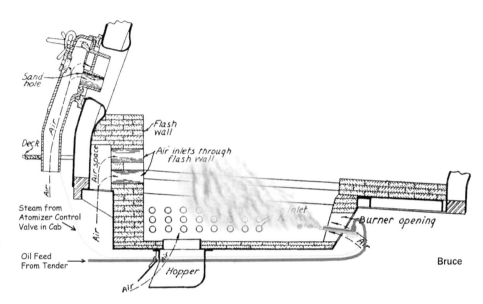

The illustration below shows a cross section of a typical U.S. style oil burner, as developed by the Southern Pacific railroad, showing how oil and steam flow through it.

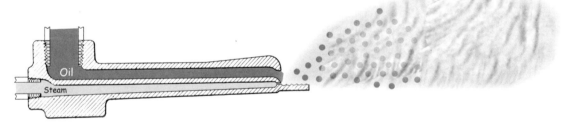

Shown below is a Southern Pacific 4-8-4, a typical oil burning locomotive. Visually, there is little to distinguish it from a coal burner, the most obvious difference being the presence of an oil tank rather than a coal bunker in the tender. If you look closely, you can often note the absence of the ash pan as well.

29

Technical Details: Train Resistance, Tractive Effort, Horsepower and Furnace Volume

The pulling power required of a locomotive is determined by the resistance of the train to movement – the force (usually measured in pounds) necessary to get the train moving and to accelerate it to the desired speed. For historical reasons, this resistance is usually expressed in terms of pounds per ton of trailing weight, so to determine the total force required to move the train you need to multiply the resistance in pounds per ton by the total weight of the train in tons, including both the weight of the loads and the weight of the cars themselves. Johnson gives a formula for train resistance

Eq. 1: $R\ (lbs/T) = 1.3 + G + 29/w + 0.045 \times V + 0.0005 \times A \times V^2 / w \times n$

Where

G is the gradient of the track, in percent

w is the average weight per axle

n is the number of axles per car

V is the speed in mph

A is the cross sectional area of a typical car, usually in the range of 85 to 90 ft²

Applying this formula to a couple of typical trains, a 4,500 T manifest (fast freight) and a 10,000 T coal drag, both on level track, gives the following values:

Speed (mph)	Resistance - Manifest (pounds)	Resistance - Coal (pounds)
0	14,531	26,957
10	16,884	31,969
20	19,893	38,020
30	23,560	45,109
40	27,883	53,236
50	32,863	62,402
60	38,500	72,606

Historically, railroads have emphasized tractive effort, the pulling force a locomotive can exert, as the primary performance metric for a steam locomotive. Tractive effort was usually expressed as "starting" tractive effort, the force the locomotive could exert when starting a train. As the train's speed increased, the tractive effort decreased, due to the fixed relationship between tractive effort, speed, and horsepower. To understand this, we need to delve into a little beginning physics.

Force is the ability to move, and more specifically accelerate, a mass. In your high school science class, you probably learned the metric units for force, Newtons, where one Newton is the force required to accelerate a mass of one kilogram by one meter per second per second. Railroads, on the other hand, used the English system of units, where a force of one pound is the force that will accelerate a mass of one pound by thirty two feet per second per second, the acceleration of gravity. The work done in moving an object (a train, for example) is the force needed to move that object multiplied by the distance it is moved. In English units, work is measured in foot-pounds. Power is the rate at which work is done, or foot-pounds per second. Historically, power was measured in units of "horsepower", which was based on the rate that a horse could work. One horsepower is equal to 1.467 ft-lbs/sec. It is clear that another way of defining power is as the product of force times speed, and it is this definition that is most useful in the context of assessing locomotive performance. Converting to units that are more useful in this context, the relationship between power, force, and speed is given by the formula

Eq. 2a: Power (HP) = Force (lbs) × Speed (mph) / 375

Or, stating it another way

Eq. 2b: Force (lbs) = 375 × Power (HP) / Speed (mph)

Or, still another way

Eq. 2c: Speed (mph) = 375 × Power (HP) / Force (lbs)

And this is the formula that we will base our discussion on.

Coming back now to steam locomotives, the maximum tractive effort of a locomotive is determined by the boiler pressure, the cylinder, driving wheel, and rod dimensions, and by the weight on the driving wheels, but can never exceed about 25% of the weight on the drivers because the coefficient of friction for steel on steel is about 25%. The maximum horsepower of a locomotive is determined primarily by the furnace volume, the volume of the firebox and combustion chamber, with many other factors, including feed water heat, superheat, steam passage geometry, valve size and geometry, valve operation, and exhaust nozzle design, making secondary contributions.

As can be seen in Figure 1, at low speeds, the tractive effort of a locomotive, the load it could pull, was limited by the adhesion of the steel wheel on the steel rail, about 25% of the weight on the drivers, hence the flat TE curve in this region. At higher speeds, the tractive effort is limited by the power the boiler can produce, as indicated in Equation2b, above, and thus drops as the speed increases. This chart also shows the effect of higher power on TE – the tractive effort at speeds above the adhesion limit speed is directly proportional to the power of the boiler.

The two curves graphically illustrate the difference between a superpower locomotive and an earlier, non-superpower, design. The C&O K-3a is an excellent non-superpower 2-8-2 while the C&O K-4 is a comparable superpower design. The two locomotives have almost the same weight on drivers and rated tractive effort (aside from the booster on the K-4) and yet at all speeds the K-4, with its greater horsepower, has significantly more tractive effort. This curve also shows the effect of the booster on the K-4 on the overall tractive effort.

To better put this chart in context, lets superimpose train resistance on these graphs. Now we can see how the higher horsepower locomotive can handle a given train as a significantly higher speed, or conversely, handle a significantly heavier train at the same speed. This distinction carries over from level track to pulling a train on a grade as well, as shown in figure 3.

The relationship between the boiler's power potential and its furnace volume has not been clear in the literature, where much more emphasis has been placed on such factors as the grate area and the total heating surface. Based on HP data measured by the railroads and reported in the technical literature and collected by Dick Dawson, this relationship can be seen in Figure 4. While the fit may not look particularly good, it is in fact much better than fits taken against other factors such as grate area, heating surface, etc.

The variations of the data points about the line can be accounted for by a variety of factors, including the fact that the measurements were taken by a variety of railroads with differing dynamometer cars and differing test practices

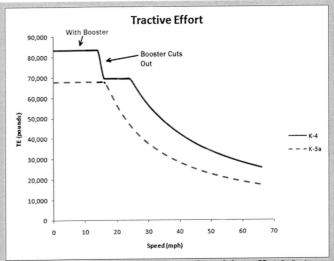

Figure 1: Tractive Effort vs. Speed for a K-4 2-8-4 and a K-3a 2-8-2

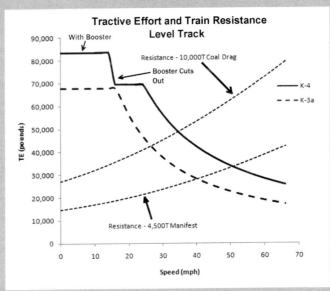

Figure 2: Tractive Effort and Train Resistance – Level Track

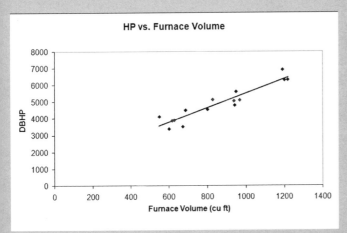

Figure 4: Locomotive Horsepower vs. Furnace Volume for a Number of Tested Locomotives.

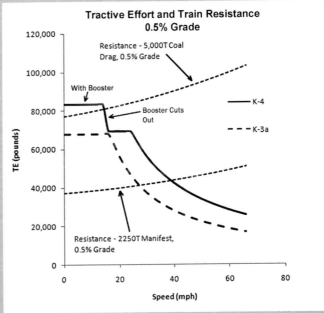

Figure 3: Tractive Effort and Train Resistance – 0.5% Grade

Exhaust and Drafting

The exhaust steam is directed through an exhaust nozzle in the bottom of the smokebox and up through the stack. In the process it pulls air and combustion gasses through the tubes and flues, creating the draft that supports combustion in the firebox. The nice thing about this arrangement is that it is self regulating – the harder the locomotive works, the more exhaust, and thus the greater the air flow through the fire, thereby increasing the fire's intensity and the amount of steam generated. For times when the locomotive is not moving, a blower is installed to provide steam flow up the stack and thus create a draft.

Note that drafting is not "free"; the required energy comes at the expense of higher back pressure in the cylinders.

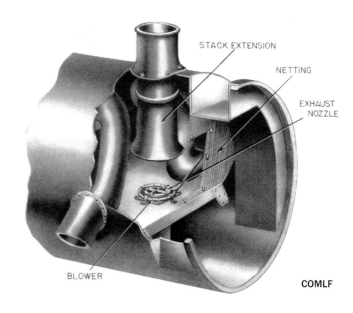

COMLF

Superheating

The superheater adds heat to the steam by routing it through superheater elements or tubes in the flues. In the Type E superheater shown here, the steam passes through two separate flues in series, with its temperature increasing by about 250°F. The earlier Type A superheater only passed the steam through one flue, and provided 150°F of superheat.

This significantly increases the overall efficiency of the locomotive, adding about 20% to 25% to the power of the locomotive as compared to the same locomotive without a superheater.

COMLF

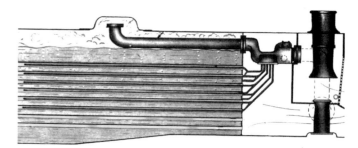

The Superheater Company

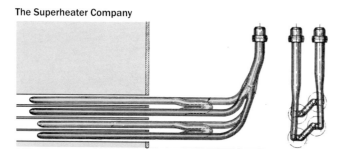

COMLF

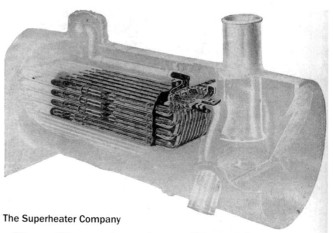

The Superheater Company

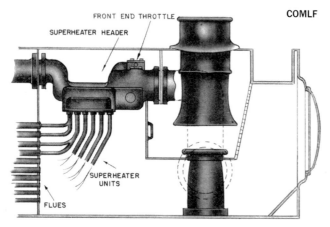

These illustrations show a "Type E" superheater, which differs from the earlier "Type A" in that it routes the steam through two smaller flues rather than one large one, and has a great many more superheater elements and boiler flues, resulting in a higher superheat. Another significant improvement of the Type E superheater over the Type A was that the throttle is located in the superheater header rather than in the dome at the opening of the dry pipe. Because of this, superheated steam rather than saturated steam is throttled.

The photo at the right shows the front of a locomotive under construction. In it you can see the front tube sheet, which holds the front ends of the tubes and flues. You can also see the superheater units inserted into the flues, and the steam delivery pipes from the front end throttle to the piston valve chambers.

The photo below shows the external linkage for the front end throttle, a rod running from the cab, through an expansion compensator, to the throttle in the smokebox.

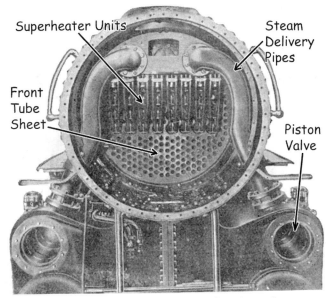

Superheater Units
Steam Delivery Pipes
Front Tube Sheet
Piston Valve

The Superheater Company

Technical Details: Superheating, Tractive Effort, Horsepower, and Efficiency

First introduced around 1905, the superheater was almost surely the most significant improvement in steam locomotive technology in the 20th Century. How else could you get as much as a 20% increase in drawbar horsepower and more than a 45% increase in tractive effort at road speed, essentially for free?

To understand what a superheater does, we first need to understand how the inherent energy, the enthalpy or heat content, in the steam varies with temperature. The top figure shows the heat content of water as it is heated to its boiling point of 404 °F at 245 psi (sometimes referred to as "psig", or gauge pressure, meaning pressure above normal atmospheric pressure of 14.7 psi.). You can see that the heat content increases as the water in the boiler is heated from ambient temperature up to the boiling point. The vertical rise is the heat of vaporization, the energy necessary to vaporize the water into steam. On a non-superheated, or saturated, locomotive, that is the heat content of the steam. The work that can be extracted from the steam is the difference in the heat content of the live steam and the heat content of the exhaust steam, which is typically saturated steam at about 25 psig. A superheater adds additional heat to the steam, increasing its energy content even further. This additional heat is then available to do work, specifically moving the locomotive and train. .

The net result of superheating is that the engine is capable of significantly more work without burning any additional fuel or evaporating any additional water. The chart shows a typical result, where superheating a locomotive increased its horsepower by 20% and its tractive effort at 34 mph by 48%.

As explained in the main text, this magic is performed by running saturated steam through pipes in the boiler's flues, capturing heat from the fire's exhaust gases that would otherwise go up the stack and be lost. This increases the locomotive's overall efficiency, the ratio of the work done to the energy released by the burning coal. This increase in efficiency can then be used in one of two different ways

To do more work (i.e. develop and use more horsepower and tractive effort) for the same amount of fuel burned, or

To do the same amount of work while burning less fuel.

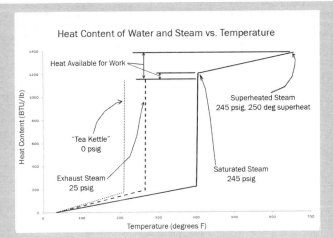

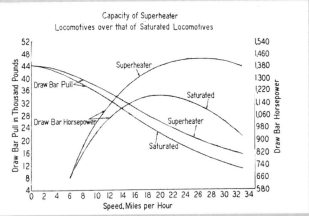

Being almost fanatically focused on efficiency, railroads initially used superheaters as a way to save operational cost, but by the 1920s the need for more power was clear, and superheating came into its own as a key component in the design of a modern locomotive.

Technical Details: Where Does the Energy Go?

It has long been known that the energy (work) you get at the drawbar of a steam locomotive's tender is a small fraction of the energy content of the coal (or other fuel) fed into the firebox. The question is, where does all the energy in the coal go? To answer that question, we must first understand the answer to a related question: why does the efficiency of the boiler appear to drop as the firing rate increases? Specifically, it was long known that the amount of steam produced at high firing rates did not account for all the heat content in the coal – it seemed as if as the firing rate increased it took more and more coal to boil the same amount of water.

This inconsistency was definitively answered in 1925 by locomotive designer and engineer Lawford H. Fry, who showed that significant energy was being lost in the form of unburned fuel blowing out the stack – in essence the black smoke that is so familiar is black because it contains a substantial amount of coal that has never been burned. The reason this happens, in essence, is that as the locomotive works harder, the draft in the smokebox increases, increasing the speed of the air flowing into the firebox through the grates. As this air flow increases, it begins to pick up small particles of coal and carry them out of the firebox, through the flues, and up the stack before they have a chance to burn. At very high output levels, this can account for almost half of the coal fed into the firebox. Other, minor, sources of heat loss in the firebox include the heat carried away by the air and combustion gasses, which are substantially hotter than the surrounding air, and the heat carried away by radiation from the firebox and boiler to the outside. Whatever is left goes into making steam and superheating it.

Once the steam is made, there are other sources of energy loss. By far the most significant is the heat of vaporization carried away by the exhaust steam. As discussed previously, a very substantial amount of heat, 970 BTUs per pound, is required to boil water into steam. This heat is never recovered since the steam is never condensed back into liquid water, and the heat lost thereby can account for upwards of 90% of the heat content of the steam, or 40% of the heat content of the coal fired. Other, less significant sources of loss are the energy expended by the exhaust steam in the smokebox to create the draft, and the energy necessary to account for friction in the mechanism and in pulling the tender.

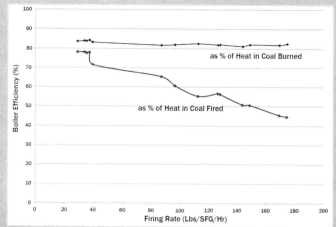

Above: Boiler efficiency as a function of firing rate (pounds of coal per square ft. of grate area per hour).

Below: Energy balance chart for a PRR L1s Mikado, at maximum output, showing where the energy contained in the fuel goes.

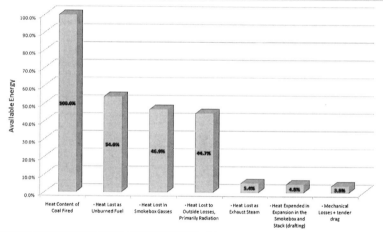

When all is said and done, only between 3% and 4% of the total energy in the coal fed into the firebox is captured as mechanical energy at the tender drawbar available to pull a train.

The following table summarizes the various energy losses for a typical locomotive being worked very hard, and is based on data on a PRR L1s Mikado, presented by Fry.

Energy Loss Source	% of remaining energy	% of energy content of coal fired	Available Energy Remaining as % of Coal Fired
Heat Lost as Unburned Fuel	46.00%	46.00%	54.0%
Heat Lost in Smokebox Gasses	13.15%	7.10%	46.9%
Heat Lost to Outside Losses, Primarily Radiation	4.69%	2.20%	44.7%
Heat Lost as Exhaust Steam	87.92%	39.30%	5.4%
Heat Expended in Expansion in the Smokebox and Stack (drafting)	12.04%	0.65%	4.8%
Mechanical Losses + tender drag	20.00%	0.95%	3.8%

PRR L1s 2-8-2 #3848, essentially a twin of the locomotive whose test results on the Altoona test plant gave rise to the energy balance figures on the facing page.

C&O H-8 2-6-6-6 #1603 at Tuckahoe, W.Va. Locomotives of this class produced the most horsepower of any reciprocating steam locomotive, due in large part to its very large fire-box and combustion chamber.

Thomas W. Dixon Collection

Above: Pennsylvania Railroad Class M1a 4-8-2 #6787 illustrates the characteristic PRR Belpaire firebox.

Left Above: Soo Line Class O-20 4-8-4 #5001 at Minneapolis MN on August 24, 1941.

Left Below: New York Central Class S-2a 4-8-4 #5500, equipped with poppet valves, unlike its 25 sisters that had piston valves and Baker valve gear.

Below: a B&O 2-8-2 crosses over the NKP main line and a NKP 2-8-4.

NYC Photo

Thomas W. Dixon Collection

Above: UP 4-12-2 #9001. Close examination will reveal the center cylinder head and Gresley valve gear of this three cylinder locomotive.

Below: B&O (ex. BR&P) 4-6-2 #5260 clearly shows its ashpan and hopper in front of the trailing truck.

Part 3: The Foundation–Frame, Drivers, and Other Wheels

Just as the pistons and cylinders of the locomotive are its muscles and the firebox and boiler its heart, the frame and wheels are the skeleton. They hold the other parts of the locomotive and hold the whole assemblage on the track.

The Frame

The frame of the locomotive must support the boiler and cylinders, and must in turn rest on the driving wheels and the leading and trailing truck, and it must do so with sufficient stiffness to hold everything in its proper place, and yet with a suspension of sufficient flexibility that the locomotive is able to negotiate irregularities in the track.

This illustration of part of the frame of PM 2-8-4 #1225 shows the journal boxes which carry the axles, arranged so that they can slide up and down in slots in the frame. Each one is sprung with leaf springs, and they are interconnected with equalizers so that the weight of the locomotive is always carried properly by the wheels. Note particularly the equalizer at the front of the frame (to the right) which connects the axle journals on the two sides with the lead truck.

This is an example of a built up or bar frame, constructed of numerous separate pieces, in this case for a C&O L-2 4-6-4. This was the most common type of frame by far. Up until the late 1930s, the frame of the locomotive was built like this, a massive assembly of parts bolted together.

Beginning in the mid to late 1930s, it became possible to cast the entire locomotive frame, including the cylinders and the main air reservoir, in a single piece. This was much stronger than a fabricated frame, never got out of alignment, and eliminated several hundred parts. This particular frame is from an L&N 2-8-4, a sister locomotive to our C&O K-4, and very like the K-4's frame, except that on the K-4 the frame casting contained the main air reservoir as well. Frames of this type were very complex and massive, weighing upwards of 150,000 pounds.

Frames for articulated locomotives, whether Mallet compound or simple expansion, were essentially two separate frames of relatively conventional construction, hinged together with a tongue in socket joint. The rear engine frame is fixed to the boiler and the front engine frame is free to swivel from side to side under the boiler. Here we see the frame assembly for the front engine of a 2-6-6-6. The tongue which will connect this frame to the rear one is clearly visible.

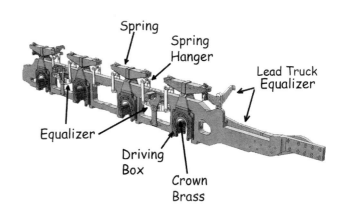

courtesy of Rod Crawford

Baldwin, COHS Collection

General Steel Castings Corporation

Lima, COHS Collection

39

Here we see the two engines of the 2-6-6-6 being brought together, making it easy to see how the two parts of the hinged joint fit together. On this engine, like many modern simple articulateds, the hinged joint only allows the front engine to swivel from side to side, with no vertical motion, relying on the springs to provide the flexibility necessary to accommodate vertical curves in the track. On many older articulated locomotives, the hinged joint allowed for some vertical motion as well.

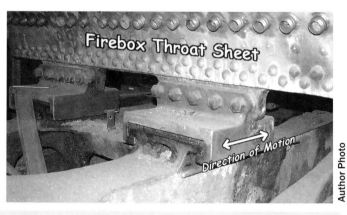

Attaching the Boiler to the Frame

One wrinkle to consider in attaching the boiler to the locomotive frame is that the boiler expands in length by a couple of inches as it heats up to operating temperature. To allow for this, the boiler is attached rigidly to the frame at the front and by means of a longitudinal sliding mount at the back to allow for this. This photo shows those longitudinally sliding supports.

This photo shows where the mounting points for C&O 2744 are located. Note that there are also waist supports above the drivers, made from flat sheets of steel, allowing them to flex as the boiler expands and contracts.

Sliding support here allows boiler to move back to front

Boiler is fixed to frame here

The boiler mounting for an articulated locomotive is a bit more complicated, because allowance must be made for the front engine to swing from side to side under the boiler. Because of this, the boiler is rigidly mounted to the rear engine frame above the rear cylinders. There is a set of longitudinally sliding supports under the firebox to allow for the boiler's expansion and contraction, and laterally sliding support above the front engine to allow for its side-to-side movement.

Longitudinally sliding support here allows the boiler to move back to front

Boiler is fixed to frame here

Laterally sliding support here allows the front engine to swing side to side under the boiler

Driving Wheels and Rods

The driving wheels are the "legs" of the locomotive; through them the force that moves the locomotive and its train is transmitted to the track. Most steam locomotives used spoked driving wheels, including our C&O 2-8-4, and the C&O 4-6-4s, to which these drivers belong.

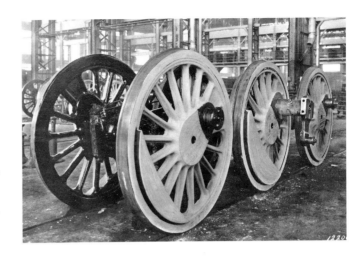

Note the counterweights, which are used to balance the weight of the connecting rods so the drivers don't pound the rail as they rotate. The counter weights were hollow so that the precise amount of weight (usually lead) could be added to achieve optimum balance. The counter weight on the main driver is larger because it must balance the weight of the main rod as well as of the side rods.

Drivers also came in a variety of other designs, including the familiar Boxpox (pronounced "box spoke"), shown here on a C&O 4-8-4, which were intended to be stronger than the spoked wheels, but many locomotives continued to use the spoked drivers up until the end of steam.

Another feature that you can easily see in this photo is that the side or connecting rods only connect a pair of drivers – there is a separate rod to connect each pair. Also, in this case, the locomotive is fitted with tandem rods between the second and third drivers, which better distributes the thrust from the main rod to the other drivers.

This photo shows the set of rods for one side of a 4-6-4 locomotive. The connecting rods are on the bottom and the top, with the main rod in the middle. Notice how the lower connecting rod, which will be mounted on the rear, has a clevis to receive the back end of the front connecting rod, and the two rods will be held together by a pin; this is called the "knuckle joint". These rods are equipped with plain bearings in floating bushings, which were not adjustable; they were simply replaced when worn.

The driving wheels ride in bearings in the frame. For most of the steam era these bearings were what are called plain bearings, as shown in this photo. Note how the bearing is able to slide up and down in its guideway, supported by the spring in the frame above it, and that the actual bearing surface is relatively large.

Late in the steam era, the Timken Company pioneered the use of roller bearings in steam locomotives. This photo shows such an installation on a locomotive driving wheel. The roller bearings are clearly visible on the axle, just inside each driving wheel.

Not long after roller bearings began to be used in the journals of the driving wheels, they also began to be applied to the side and main rods on the crankpin journals. This photo illustrates such an application. Note how the ends of the rods are enlarged to contain the roller bearings.

Crossheads and Crosshead Guides

In Part 1 we looked at the piston and its rod, and in this section we've looked at the rods that connect the wheels to each other and to the piston. The connection point between the upper end of the main rod and the piston rod is the crosshead. There are several common types of crossheads. Early in the steam era, the Laird crosshead was quite popular. You can recognize this type by the "slot" that the crosshead rides in.

Later on, the Alligator crosshead became popular. This type is easily identified by having guides both above and below the crosshead itself.

While the Laird and Alligator crossheads remained in common use, many if not most modern steam locomotives are equipped with the Multiple Bearing crosshead, so called because it provides several bearing surfaces between the crosshead and guide to better carry the forces exerted by the high thrust of the piston. The sketch below shows how the top of the crosshead has a set of flanges that fit into corresponding groves in the guide to provide the multiple bearing surfaces.

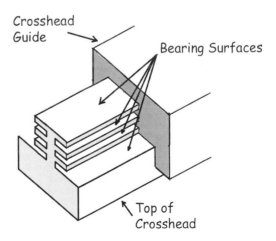

Technical Details: Counterbalancing

A major issue in the design of a locomotive's running gear is how to counteract the oscillations induced by the weight of the propulsion machinery oscillating back and forth and around and around.

The weight of the cranks, crank pins, and connecting rods on the driving wheels causes the drivers on each side of the locomotive to experience a wobble, just as an out of balance tire on an automobile will wobble. This wobble affects the performance of the locomotive by causing a vertical force, called "dynamic augment", that oscillates up and down as the wheel turns, which can affect the locomotive's traction and in extreme cases can cause damage to the track. When the vertical oscillations from both sides of the locomotive are combined, the result is that the entire locomotive tends to rock from side to side. The magnitude of these forces, and the resultant rocking increases with the square of the rotational speed of the drivers.

This vertical oscillation can be essentially eliminated by adding a counter weight to the driving wheel, sized and positioned to balance out the weight of the crank, pin, and rod. These weights are usually made of lead and are housed in compartments cast into the wheel near the rim, opposite the crankpin. As locomotives got heavier, with heavier rods, and their speeds got higher, it became difficult to fit enough weight into the counterweight pockets to balance the locomotive. The basic solution was to make the driving wheels bigger, which helped in two ways. First, the rotational speed of the larger drivers was less for a given track speed than for smaller drivers. Second, larger drivers allowed the counterweights to be placed further from the wheel center, increasing their effectiveness and decreasing the weight needed to balance the wheels. The downside, of course, is that larger drivers decrease the tractive effort of the locomotive, and decrease the space available for the boiler within the railroad's clearance limits. The use of high strength steel, first available in the 1930s, helped too by allowing the rods to be lighter in weight for the same strength, decreasing the weight needed to balance them.

Even if each side of a pair of drivers is balanced for its own crank, pin, and rod, there is some residual side to side rocking oscillation caused by the fact that the counterweight and rods are in two different planes, causing a slight wobble. This is exacerbated by the fact that the two drivers are quartered rather than being either aligned or exactly out of step with each other. Late in the steam age, this residual rocking was remedied by "cross-counter balancing" the entire driver pair. This is accomplished by moving the counter weight on each side slightly away from being exactly opposite from the crankpin, and resulted in a driver pair that did not rock back and forth at high speeds.

The back and forth oscillation of the pistons, piston rods, crosshead, and main rod causes the entire locomotive to nose from side to side as it moves down the track, causing significant wear on both the locomotive and the track structure. Locomotive engineers recognized this effect early in the history of locomotive development and devised any number of schemes to attempt to balance out this side to side oscillation, all centered on adding additional weight to the driver counter weights to balance out this side to side motion. While balancing out the wobble of an unbalanced driver is relatively straightforward, balancing the weight of the oscillating pistons and other drive machinery is a much more complicated task, one filled with compromises. It is also affected by the locomotive's wheel arrangement, since locomotives with longer rigid wheel bases are more resistant to transverse oscillations, and the locomotive's overall weight, since the heavier the locomotive is, the more resistant it is to oscillations in any direction.

One complication comes from the fact that as you add addi-

tional weight to the driver counterweights to balance the lateral oscillations, you are unbalancing the rotational balance of the drivers and reintroducing the rocking oscillations that arise from the drivers being out of rotational balance. This is generally addressed by spreading the "overbalance" out onto all the drivers, rather than concentrating it on one driver pair. The amount of weight to be added to each driver's counterweight was a carefully thought out (most of the time) compromise between the magnitude of the lateral and rocking oscillations of the locomotive, and the damage each caused to the track.

Complicating this balancing act is the fact that the main rod oscillates from front to back at its front end and rotates at its back end. Determining how much of the weight of the rod to assign to each motion was, in the days before computers and computational dynamics, a black art at best. Because it carried the weight of the main rod as well as the side rods, the counter weight on the main driver was always significantly larger than the counterweights on the other drivers. How much larger was usually determined by empirical formulas and "rules of thumb".

Another method that some railroads used to achieving balance in a locomotive was to adjust the lateral resistance of the lead truck. By stiffening up the suspension of the lead truck, it can absorb some of the force from the lateral oscillations, allowing the overbalance in the counter weights to be less, and allowing the locomotive to be closer to perfect rotational balance. The downside to this approach was that this stiffer lead truck made it more difficult to negotiate curves, particularly sharp ones. Again, this approach called for a compromise between the balance of the locomotive's running gear and the ability to negotiate tight curves.

The locomotive rocks from side to side due to rotational imbalance in the driving wheels and oscillates horizontally due to the forward and back motion of the pistons, piston rods, main rods and other parts of the mechanism.

Springing and Equalization

The driving wheel axles are not mounted rigidly to the frame since such an arrangement would not be nearly flexible enough to allow the wheels to stay on the rails over even the slightest irregularities. The wheel bearings are carried in *driving boxes* which are mounted on springs on the frame and are free to move up and down within slots in the frame, but constrained from moving from front to back. The springs are connected to each other by *equalizers* which transfer the load from one spring to another, ensuring that when one wheel set lifts, the others will stay firmly planted on the rail.

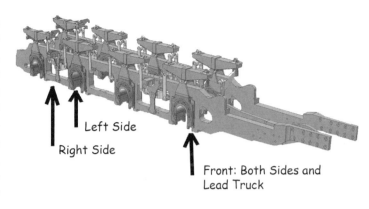

Left Side

Right Side

Front: Both Sides and Lead Truck

Courtesy of Rod Crawford

Note that the equalizers are connected in such a was as to support the locomotive on three points, like a very stable tripod. In this example, the lead truck and both sides of the first two pairs of drivers are connected, providing one leg of the tripod. The rear two drivers on each side are connected with the trailing truck wheels on the same side, providing the other two legs of the tripod.

Lead and Trailing Trucks

The purpose of the lead truck is to lead the locomotive into and out of curves in the track, and to keep the front end of the locomotive from "hunting" back and forth on straight track, as well as carry part of the locomotive's weight.

Freight locomotive tended to have two wheel lead trucks, whereas passenger locomotive tended to have four wheel (two axle) lead, or engine, trucks.

Most often engine trucks were equipped with inside bearings, but some had outside bearings like the one shown here.

Regardless of the number of axles (one or two) and location of the bearings, all engine trucks were equipped with a centering device to allow them to perform their primary function, which was to lead the locomotive into and out of curves by exerting some lateral force on the front of the locomotive.

The main function of the trailing truck was to carry the weight of the back end of the locomotive, primarily the firebox. Trailing trucks almost always had outside bearings (remember, there's an ashpan in there) and had one, two, or rarely three axles.

Rocker type weight support

Each side of the trailing truck is equalized with the drivers on that side.

The rocker type weight support was used on all modern locomotives to carry some of the boiler's weight on the trailing truck and to help keep the truck centered under the boiler. It consists of a semicircular vertical support that pivots at the bottom on the back end of the trailing truck and rests in a shallow vee-shaped recess on the locomotive frame.

Author Photo

45

Before outside bearing lead trucks were used, inside bearing trucks were used, and in fact remained in common use right up till the end of steam.

While two wheel lead trucks were commonly used on freight locomotives, passenger locomotives almost exclusively used four wheel lead trucks, which are much more stable at speed. These trucks were also used on some freight locomotives, particularly those that were intended to run at higher speeds.

In addition to inside bearings, four wheel lead trucks could be found with outside frames and bearings.

Thomas W. Dixon Collection

The first trailing trucks weren't really trucks at all, but simply smaller, non-powered wheels mounted in the locomotive frame and sometimes provide with the ability to move somewhat from side to side to accommodate curvature in the track. Almost always such trailers had the wheel bearings on the inside of the wheels.

The main purpose of these trailers, and in fact of any trailing truck, is to carry some of the locomotive's weight at the back end and to allow the firebox to be mounted behind and below the driving wheels.

The next development in the trailing wheel was to mount it in a truck that pivoted under the locomotive frame. This type of trailer would much more easily follow curves in the track. The first of these pivoted trailing trucks are built up from a large number of individual parts, as in the Cole truck shown here, which was centered under the locomotive by a transverse spring. Note the equalizer extending from the bottom of the front spring hanger forward to behind the driving wheel.

One virtue of the outside bearing trailer that is not often noted is that having the bearings on the outside leaves more room for the ashpan under the firebox.

Later trailing trucks were made from large steel castings, as in the Delta truck shown here, making them much stronger and also much less maintenance intensive.

You can just see the end of the equalizer in the opening in front of the journal box.

An early type of four wheel trailing truck was the Lima Articulated Backend. This unit replaced the frame under the firebox and supported the entire back of

the locomotive as well as providing the anchor for the tender drawbar. In this photo you can clearly see how the locomotive frame ends directly in front of the trailing truck. This truck was commonly used on early Super Power locomotives, particularly those built by Lima, but by 1930 or so had been supplanted by the four wheel Delta type truck used on our C&O 2-8-4.

As the sizes of locomotives increased, they eventually reached the point where a two wheel truck could not support all the weight, and the four wheel truck was developed. At the very end of the age of steam, a few locomotives exceeded the size that a four wheel truck could handle and the six wheel trailing truck came into being. Other than two unique PRR locomotives, this truck was only used on the 60 C&O and 8 VGN 2-6-6-6s.

Pilots

Sometimes called a "cow catcher" the pilot performs two main functions: to prevent objects (including people) from being run over by the locomotive by shoving them out of the way, and to provide some sort of step for trainmen to use to both climb up onto and to ride on the locomotive. Several types of pilots were common.

This is a common pilot on switching locomotives – just footboards.

This is a common freight and passenger locomotive pilot, with slats fabricated from used boiler tubes or flat bars.

Many modern freight locomotives had pilots similar to this one, fabricated from castings bolted together.

Many modern passenger locomotives and some freight locomotives had pilots of this sort, with retractable couplers. In this case, hiding the front coupler prevents an automobile from being impaled on the front of the locomotive in the event of a grade crossing accident, allowing the pilot to push the auto to the side.

Above: B&A class A-1a 2-8-4 #1415 displays its Lima Articulated Back-End at Worcester, Mass.

Below: Other than on subsidiaries Boston and Albany and Pittsburgh and Lake Erie, the New York Central did not use the popular Berkshire (2-8-4) type for fast freight service, relying instead on several classes of very modern Mountain (4-8-2) types. Shown here is one of the newest, L4a #3101, built by Lima in 1941.

Thomas W. Dixon collection

Left: B&O class Q-4 2-8-2 #4444. Note the long frame Baker valve gear, Alligator cross-head, Delta type outside bearing trailing truck, and side-hung air pump.

Lower Left: MP class BK-63 2-8-4 #1922 at St. Louis, Mo. in June, 1938. Prominent are the outside bearing lead truck and the Worthington BL type feedwater heater hung on the side of the locomotive. The displaced air pumps are mounted on the pilot deck, behind a pair of shields. The cylindrical object on top of the smokebox in front of the stack is the casing for a front end throttle, in this case one that is not integrated with the superheater header. Note too the small door on the side of the tender, behind which is mounted the stoker engine.

Below: Baldwin builder's photo of RF&P "General" class 4-8-4 #553 in 1937. Note the conical housings on the outer faces of the lead truck wheels – these are characteristic of roller bearings on Baldwin locomotives.

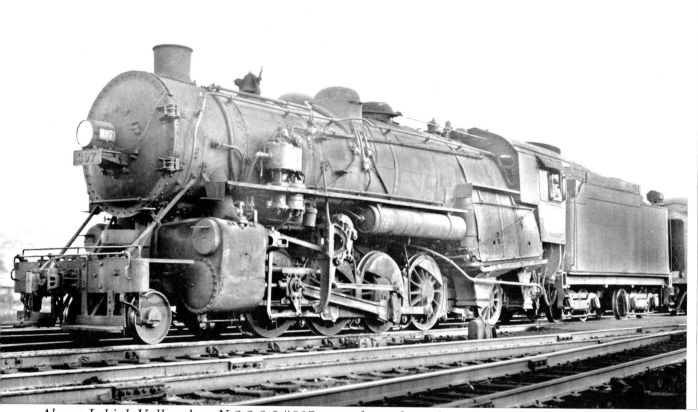

Above: Lehigh Valley class N-2 2-8-2 #397 wears her ashpan hoppers on the outside in addition to the one inside, to accommodate the extra wide grate of the Wooten firebox. This wider than usual firebox is characteristic of locomotives designed to use slow burning anthracite coal.

Below: Northern Pacific 4-8-4 #2601's trailing truck is surrounded by a "banjo" frame extension that allowed extra room for the ashpan, necessary because of the high ash content of the "Rosebud" semi-bituminous coal used by this road.

Above: Virginian Railway Class AG 2-6-6-6 # 906 at Norfolk, Va. in July, 1948. VGN bought these copies of the successful C&O original, but had them built with smaller sandboxes since they were not intended to cross the Allegheny mountains but instead to run on the low grade route from Roanoke to Norfolk.

Below: L&N 4-8-2 #402 at Cincinnati, Ohio, in September, 1938. Note the Cole outside bearing trailing truck on this handsome locomotive.

New Haven 4-6-2 #1355 proudly displays her Elesco feedwater heater on top of her smokebox.

Part 4: Auxiliaries–Stoker, Feedwater, Air Pumps, etc.

Stokers

As locomotives got bigger their demand for fuel exceeded the ability of one and even two firemen to supply with shovels. The solution to this dilemma was the mechanical stoker, consisting of a screw coal conveyer that moved the coal from the tender to a firing table just inside the firebox, where it was scattered around the firebox by steam jets.

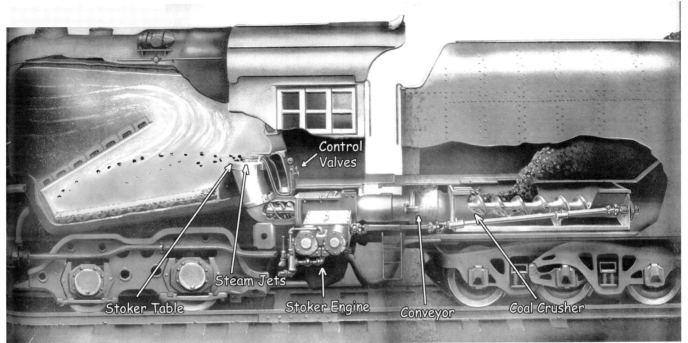

all, COMLF

Here you can see a typical firing table, with a number of steam jet ports visible, and the coal distribution pattern that results from its use. This particular stoker has five separately controllable jets, set up to spray coal in a fan shaped pattern. Each jet has a separate control valve, allowing the fireman to control the distribution of coal throughout the firebox.

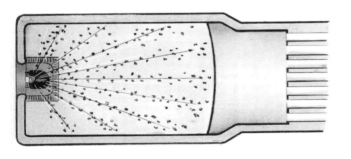

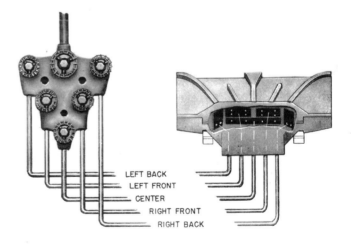

This illustration shows the steam jets on the firing table and the array of valves that control the jets.

The stoker's conveyer screws are driven by a small two cylinder steam engine, usually located under the cab floor on the fireman's (left) side, although it was sometimes placed in the front of the tender instead. There were typically two screws, one in the bottom of the tender's coal space, another under the cab floor, which also pushed the coal up to the firing table. The screw in the tender was fitted with steel "teeth" to allow it to break up large chunks of coal into a size that could be carried through the conveyer to the firebox.

The fireman regulated the fuel flow by regulating the steam supply to and thus the speed of the stoker engine.

The stoker engine was commonly located under the cab floor on the fireman's (left) side of the locomotive or in a compartment in the front of the tender.

Note that the stoker illustrated here was the most popular of a number of different, competing designs.

Smoke Consumers

The purpose of the smoke consumer (a.k.a over-fire jets) was to introduce extra air into the firebox just above the firebed and thus induce turbulence in the air above the firebed. This ensured thorough mixing of the air and the burning fuel and complete combustion of all the fuel before it entered the tubes and flues where it stopped burning because of rapid cooling.

These most commonly used the Bernoulli effect whereby a jet of steam was used to draw air into the firebox, much like an paint sprayer uses a jet of air to draw paint up from its reservoir and spray it.

There were several designs of smoke consumers, mostly varying by the presence and specific design of a noise muffler.

Sadly, the extra efficiency gained by more complete combustion was partially offset by the cooling effect of introducing (relatively) cold outside air into the firebox.

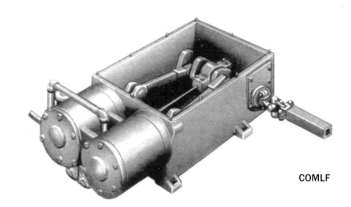

COMLF

COMLF

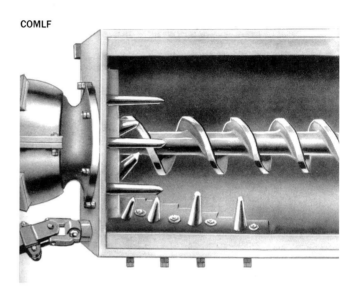

Injectors

All steam locomotives were required to have two independent ways of getting water into the boiler. Some were equipped with two injectors, others with a feedwater heater of some sort and one injector. In many cases on older locomotives that didn't have feedwater heaters, the injectors were located out of sight in the cab. On locomotives equipped with feedwater heaters, the injector was commonly located under the cab on the engineer's (right) side.

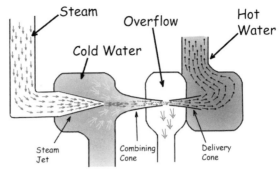

The injector uses the Bernoulli effect to put water into the boiler. A jet of live steam is passed in front of a water supply, which it carries forward and into the boiler, much like a paint spray gun. In the process the steam expands and condenses, and the energy released thereby heats the water, commonly to between 250°F and 300°F, as well as pressurizing it so that it can flow into the boiler against the boiler pressure. The combination of expanding steam from the boiler, the Bernoulli effect, and recovering the heat of vaporization results in tremendous force to move the water into the boiler. The hot water is fed into the boiler through a check valve which allows water to flow into the boiler but not out.

Note that there were two type of injectors, lifting and non-lifting. The lifting injector creates a partial vacuum and can lift the cold water from the tender above the tender water level. The non-lifting injector cannot, and must rely on gravity for the cold water feed. Because of this, all of the energy in the steam is used to heat and pressurize the water, making the non-lifting injector more efficient. Non-lifting injectors also are able to deliver more water to the boiler, an important consideration for a large locomotive.

This photo shows a lifting injector, which can lift water above the water level in the tender, hence its placement high on the side of the boiler.

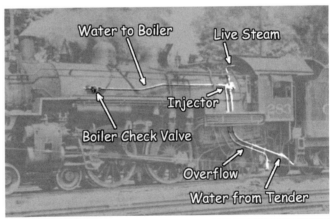

This photo shows a typical non-lifting injector as installed on a modern steam locomotive. Note that, unlike the lifting injector in the photo above, the injector body is located very low, essentially at the level of the tender bottom, because this injector is not able to lift water from the tender and must rely on gravity to feed water from the tender to the injector. Note the live steam delivery pipe coming down from the turret and the hot water delivery pipe leading forward to the boiler check valve just in front of the sand dome.

Feedwater Heaters

While the injector is a very effective device for increasing the temperature of the boiler feed water and for forcing it into the boiler against the boiler pressure, it has the disadvantage of using live steam fairly inefficiently. Consequently, other devices were developed to do the same job. What developed was the *feed water heater*, which uses exhaust steam to heat the cold water from the tender and pumps to force the water into the boiler. While it doesn't heat the water as much as an injector, only to between 150°F and 200°F, its use of exhaust steam, energy that would otherwise be lost, to heat the water (and pumps to force the water into the boiler) means that the heater's use favorably impacts locomotive power output. Its use increases both overall efficiency and peak horsepower output by about 10%.

Feedwater heaters come in two basic types, open and closed. In the open type, the exhaust steam comes into direct contact with the feed water, whereas in the closed type, they are kept separate. These two figures show schematically how the two types work.

In the open type, exhaust steam passes through the settling chamber, where lubricating oil from the cylinders is separated from the steam, and then into the mixing chamber. In the mixing chamber, cold water is sprayed, condensing the steam and picking up heat in the process. The resulting hot water is pumped into the boiler.

In the closed type, exhaust steam fills the outer part of the heater barrel, while cold water flows through a bundle of tubes within the barrel to be heated by the steam.

Because of the break in the water circuit at the mixing chamber, the open type requires two separate pumps, one for cold water and one for hot. The closed type, on the other hand, only requires one pump since there is no break in the water circuit. Both types worked well, with the complexity of the open type's second pump somewhat offset by its somewhat greater efficiency and the complexity of the closed type heater.

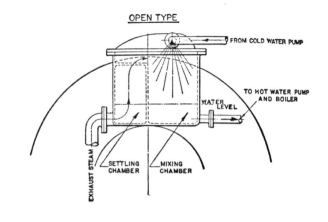

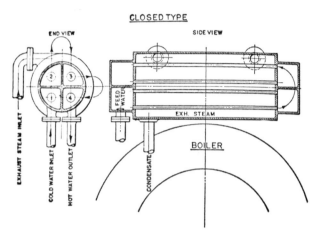

both, Bruce

Worthington SA: In this open type heater commonly used from the mid-1920s on, the cold water pump pumps water from the tender to the heater unit in the smokebox in front of the stack. Inside the heater unit, exhaust steam is mixed with cold water from the tender, heating it almost to boiling temperature. The hot water pump above the crosshead then pumps this hot water into the boiler.

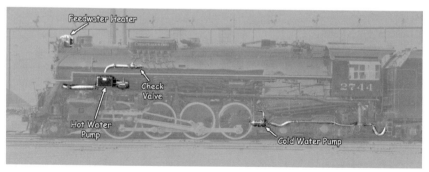

Elesco: In this closed system the exhaust steam is not mixed with the cold water, rather the heater body is filled with exhaust steam and the cold water is run through bundles of small tubing inside the heater, where the water is heated by the surrounding steam. Because there is no open space in the water circuit, the same pump that moves the water from the tender to the heater can also pump the water into the boiler.

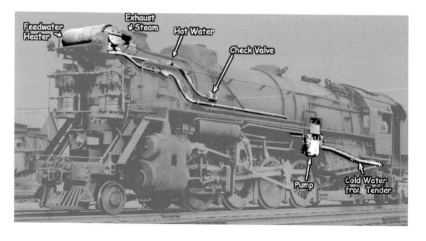

Worthington BL: This older type of open system is similar to the Worthington SA type heater in that exhaust steam is mixed with tender water to heat it. In this version, the heating chamber and both the cold water and hot water pumps are integrated into one massive unit.

Because of this and the constraints that this design places on the overall size of the heater, the BL type heater has a smaller capacity than the more modern SA type design.

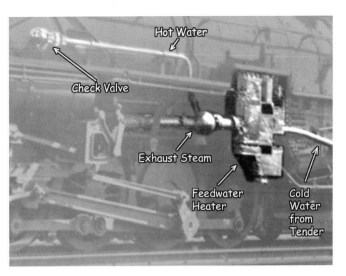

Low Water Alarm

This device works by keeping the expansion tube filled with water from the boiler, which cools off since it's not circulating through the boiler. Should the water level in the boiler fall too low, the water in the tube would drain out, the tube will fill with steam, heat up, and expand, closing the contact studs and setting off an alarm whistle.

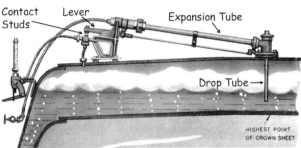

Technical Details: the Bernoulli Effect and Its Application to Locomotive Appliances

The Bernoulli principle states that as the speed of a fluid (gas or liquid) increases, its pressure decreases. The Bernoulli effect makes use of this fact to use a fast moving stream of fluid to induce motion in fluid that is not moving, taking advantage of the pressure differential that exists between the moving and non-moving fluids.

For example, a common paint sprayer directs a jet of air across the top of a tube whose bottom end is immersed in a liquid, paint for example. Because of the air jet, the air pressure at the top of the tube is lower than the surrounding air pressure, which pushes paint up through the tube and into the air jet, where it is atomized (broken into small droplets) and carried along.

This same principal is applied to a number of steam locomotive appliances. These include:

The exhaust nozzle and stack, where the exhaust steam from the cylinders is forced through a nozzle to increase its speed and then up through the stack. In the area between the mouth of the nozzle and the mouth of the stack the exhaust steam jet creates a region of lower pressure that pulls air through the tubes and flues of the boiler, and hence through the firebed.

Similarly, the blower supplies jets of boiler steam from a set of small nozzles set around the exhaust nozzle when the locomotive is not moving, creating the same effect.

In the injector a jet of steam creates a low pressure area which draws water along, forcing it into the boiler.

Smoke consumers use a jet of steam to capture some of the surrounding air and force it into the firebox.

Blow Down

Any water contains insoluble minerals and other particulates. This material will collect in the lowest point in the boiler, and must be cleaned out, a process called blowing down.

The hot water and sludge is drained from the lowest point in the boiler, run through a muffler on the top of the boiler. Steam and the water carrying the sediment are separated, and then the water is discharged onto the track.

This view of a boiler under construction (in this case a C&O H-8 Allegheny) shows the two blow down cocks located at the lowest point in the boiler, right at the front of the firebox at the bottom. This is where sediment and precipitated minerals will settle first and thus is the best place to drain them out.

This photo shows the muffler on the top of the boiler, just in front of the cab.

The inset photo shows the discharge tube, located just behind the right rear driver.

Sanding

Our C&O K-4 carried about 6,000 pounds (3 tons) of sand in the sandbox on top of the boiler. When extra traction was needed, sand could be put on the rail just ahead of each driving wheel, coming down from the sandbox through small pipes.

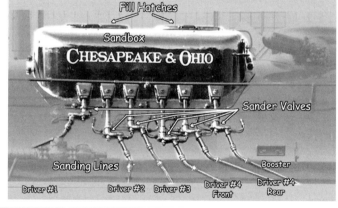

Note that on this engine, sanding pipes are provided for each driving wheel for forward motion, plus another for the booster wheels, and yet another on the rear axle only for reverse movement.

Booster

The booster is a small two cylinder steam engine geared to the rear axle of the trailing truck. This allows some of the weight on the trailing truck to be used for traction.

The typical booster was only good up to perhaps 20 mph or so, and then was mechanically disengaged from the axle by means of the idler gear and shut off, both to conserve steam, which the booster used in significant amounts, and to save on wear and tear on the booster engine itself. Some boosters used on passenger engines were usable up to 30 or even 35 mph.

Franklin Railway Supply Company

The photos below show the plumbing for the booster's steam supply, on the right side of the locomotive, and exhaust, on the left side of the locomotive.

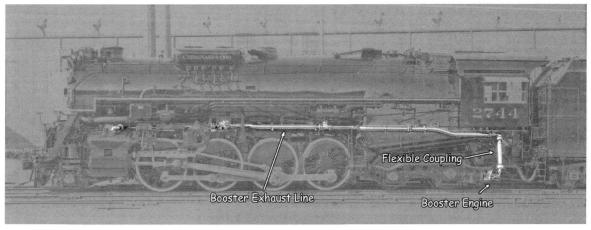

Boosters were also sometimes installed on one of the trucks on the tender, particularly on somewhat smaller engines such as the switcher shown here.

Franklin Railway Supply Company

61

Air Brakes

Like freight cars, the steam locomotive was equipped with air brakes, albeit with a much more complex installation than the typical freight car.

The locomotive is responsible for providing all the air to operate the air brakes on the train, and thus requires one or more air pumps and air reservoirs. Our K-4, like many modern locomotives, has two cross-compound air pumps mounted on either side of the pilot deck. K-4s 2700 – 2739 had three air tanks mounted under the running boards to serve as air reservoirs. Beginning with #2740, these engines had a single large tank that was cast as an integral part of the frame.

The air brake system is designed so that the engineer can control the brakes on the locomotive separately and independently of the train brakes, so for example the brakes can be applied to the train but not on the locomotive, allowing the engineer to keep the slack in the couplers stretched out. The locomotive brakes can also be set up so that they apply and release when the engineer applies and releases the train brakes, and so that they apply and release under the control of another locomotive, for use when operating as a helper.

In both the top and middle photos, you can see one of the two air pumps and an after cooler which cools the compressed air, mounted between the two pumps. In the middle photo, a protective shield is placed in front of the pumps.

On the right is the air pumps on a Northern Pacific 4-8-4, where they were mounted on the side of the boiler. There is no after cooler in this installation – they relied on loops of pipe, which was the most common way, to cool the hot compressed air. Note too that in this photo you can see the intake air strainers, used to filter the air before it was compressed.

Perhaps more locomotives had the pumps mounted on the side of the boiler than had them mounted on the pilot deck.

Note that these pumps are "cross-compound" pumps, with a high pressure steam cylinder exhausting into a low pressure steam cylinders; and driving low and high pressure air cylinders respectively, with the air compressed in the low pressure cylinder being further compressed in the high pressure cylinder. Older single stage pumps had less pumping capacity.

Thomas W. Dixon Collection

62

The actual brakes on the locomotive consist of brake shoes on the driving wheels, hung on vertical levers between the drivers and actuated by a brake cylinder that is, at least on modern locomotives, essentially hidden. Frequently brakes were installed on the locomotive's trailing truck, but only occasionally were they installed on a leading truck, usually only on four wheel lead trucks. The tender trucks always had brakes on all wheels, and these functioned in unison with the locomotive brakes.

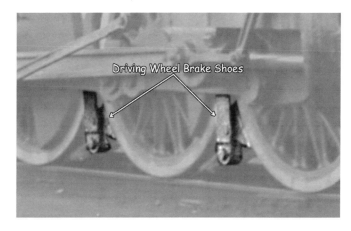

Lubrication

Many modern locomotives were fitted with automatic lubricators, usually one on each side, or sometimes, as shown here on C&O J-3 Greenbrier (4-8-4) #601, two on one side.

Each lubricator contains a different type of oil, and is driven by a link from the crosshead.

Generator, Headlight, Whistle and Bell

Until the advent of radios, the major use of electricity on a steam locomotive was lights, primarily the headlight and marker lights, but also other lights in the cab and for illuminating walkways and steps. The photo at the right shows the "conventional" location for the headlight, on the smokebox front. On the C&O at least, most of the modern locomotives had the headlight placed on the pilot deck.

The electric headlights are powered by one or more generators. These generators are powered by a small steam turbine and typically produce direct current at a relatively low voltage like 24V.

Federal railroad regulations require the use of specific whistle and bell signals, thus every locomotive must be equipped with both.

Smoke Deflectors

As steam locomotives got larger their bigger boilers began to create air currents that would pull the smoke from the stack down along the side of the boiler and into the cab, obscuring the crew's view to the front and generally making the cab an unpleasant place to be. To address this problem, the railroads tried a variety of different measures, ultimately settling on a set of plates on either side of the boiler or stack to deflect air upward and carry the smoke with it. These proved to be successful, and were adopted by many roads, particularly for high speed locomotives. The photo shows a set of "elephant ears", as they were often called, on a New York Central Mohawk (4-8-2).

Thomas W. Dixon Collection

Builder's Plates

Each of the three major builders affixed a distinctively shaped builder's plate to the smokebox of each locomotive they built, showing the locomotive's serial number and build date. These three photos show, from left to right, Baldwin's round plate, Alco's rectangular plate, and Lima's diamond shaped plate.

Two examples of smoke deflectors –

Top: Nickel Plate 4-6-4 #177 prepares to depart with a train, equipped with "mini" elephant ears around the stack.

Above: UP FEF-2 4-8-4 #824 models its very large elephant ears at North Platte, Nebraska on October 18, 1954.

Above: D&RGW Class L-105 4-6-6-4 #3704 at Helper, Utah. Note the Elesco feedwater heater, the smokebox hung air compressors, and the distinctive Baldwin roller bearing covers on the lead truck wheels.

Below: NYC class H-10a 2-8-2, at Youngstown, Ohio, ca. 1927. The large pipe on the top of the boiler behind the stack is an external dry pipe, carrying saturated steam from the dome to the superheater.

both, Thomas W. Dixon Collection

66

photo by W. Kraniec, Thomas W. Dixon Collection

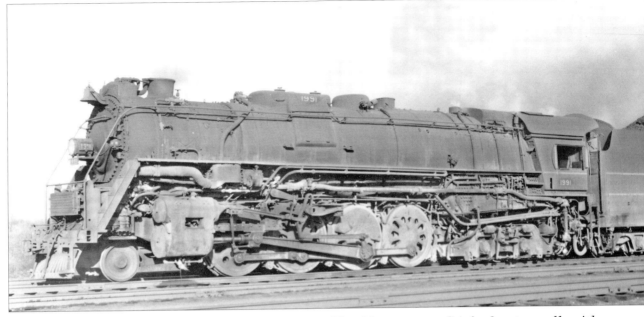

Above: L&N class M-1 2-8-4 #1991 displays her Worthington type SA feedwater well, with the hot water pump just above and behind the cylinders and the actual feedwater heater on the smokebox top just ahead of the stack.

Below: CB&Q 4-6-4 #3003, with two air pumps on the right side and an Elesco feedwater heater on the top of the smokebox. The large box behind the sandbox houses Automatic Train Control (ATC) equipment. Note that this locomotive has a Box Pox main driver and the other two drivers are spoked.

photo by C.T. Felstead, Thomas W. Dixon Collection

Above: Wabash class O-1 4-8-4 #2900. Notable are its outside bearing lead truck and its vestibule cab.

Below: UP 2-8-8-0 #3554. With the weight of the Worthington type BL feedwater heater and two cross-compound air pumps on the left side, it's a wonder it doesn't list to port.

Part 5: Cab and Controls

The Cab

The cab is where the engine crew work – its main function is to provide shelter to the crew in inclement weather. Most locomotives, including our C&O 2-8-4, had cabs that were open in the back; canvas curtains were provided to keep out bad weather.

The photo at the right shows the cab of a C&O L-2 Hudson. The cab curtains are clearly visible, as is the deckplate, which allowed the engine crew to go back and forth between the cab and the tender deck.

This photo also shows a number of the appliances we've discussed earlier, including the stoker, injector, booster, and trailing truck support.

Also visible are the drawbar and safety bar which connect the locomotive to the tender, and immediately above them the buffer and snubber which serve as cushions between the tender and the locomotive. The purpose of all this is to ensure that there is no slack between the locomotive and tender.

Some railroads, particularly those that ran in areas with extreme cold climates, used a vestibule cab which was fully enclosed, including an enclosed passage way between the cab and the tender deck, which was also enclosed, as shown here on a DM&IR Yellowstone (2-8-8-4).

Author's Collection

69

The cab of a steam locomotive presents a bewildering array of gauges, valves, and levers, many of which are not labeled as to function or purpose. Fortunately, we have illustrations like the ones on these two pages, taken from the C&O's "Manual for Locomotive Fireman", which identify them all.

Note that on this locomotive the backhead is lagged (insulated) and jacketed, making for a somewhat cooler cab. Not all railroads did this, and the back of the boiler made for a warm working environment for the engine crew, which was nice in the winter, but not so comfortable in the summer.

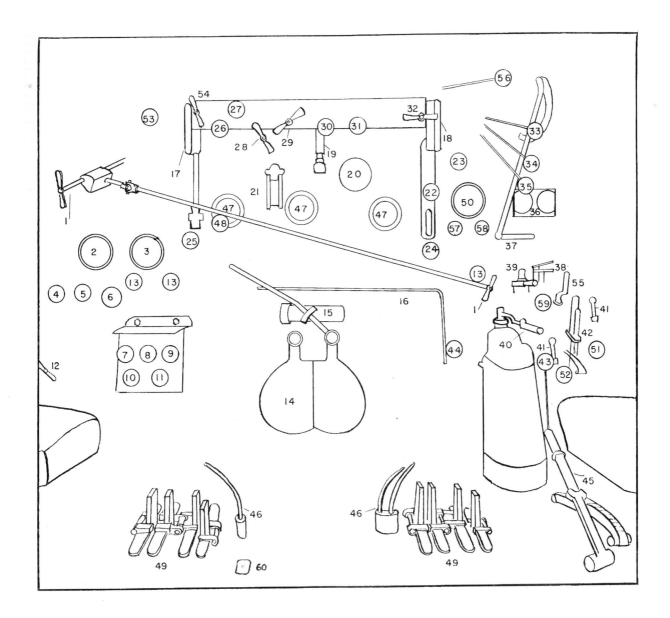

CAB INTERIOR

1. Feedwater Pump, Operating Valve Handle
2. Feedwater Pump Gauge
3. Stoker Gauge
4. Stoker Booster Valve
5. Stoker Throttle Valve
6. Stoker Intermediate Jet Control Valve
7. Left Front Stoker Distributor Valve
8. Center Stoker Distributor Valve
9. Right Front Stoker Distributor Valve
10. Left Back Stoker Distributor Valve
11. Right Back Stoker Distributor Valve
12. Blower Valve
13. Tunnel Mask Valves
14. Fire Door
15. Fire Door Cylinder
16. Firedoor Shield
17. Left Water Glass
18. Right Water Glass
19. Low Water Alarm Whistle
20. Badge Plate
21. Steam Gauge
22. Right Water Glass Drain Valve
23. Shut Off Valve for Right Water Glass
24. Water Column Drain Valve
25. Left Water Glass Drain Valve
26. Stoker Engine Valve
27. Stoker Jet Valve
28. Left Water Glass Steam Valve
29. Main Turret Valve
30. Generator Steam Valve
31. Cab Heater Valve
32. Injector Steam Valve
33. Upper Gauge Cock
34. Middle Gauge Cock
35. Lower Gauge Cock
36. Air Gauge
37. Throttle Lever
38. Whistle Valve
39. Independent Brake Valve
40. Automatic Brake Valve
41. Sander Valve
42. Power Reverse Lever
43. Rail Washer Valve
44. Firedoor Air Valve
45. Injector Operating Lever
46. Water Gauge Drain Pipes
47. Washout Plugs
48. Left Water Glass Valve
49. Grate Levers and Locks
50. Back Pressure Gauge
51. Blowdown Valve
52. Continuous Blowdown Valve
53. Feedwater Pump Operating Valve
54. Feedwater Pump Main Steam Valve
55. Cylinder Cock Operating Valve
56. Right Water Glass Steam Valve
57. Steam Chest Pressure Throttle Valve
58. Back Pressure Throttle Valve
59. Bell Ringer Valve
60. Firedoor Foot Pedal

The Steam Turret

Directly in front of the cab on the top of the boiler was the steam turret or just turret. The turret is essentially a plumbing tree of pipes and valves whose purpose is to supply steam to all the accessories that require it. In many but not all cases the turret was enclosed in a sheet metal housing. The photos below show the turret; the one on the right showing the turret with the housing opened so that the various pipes and valves are visible. The external valves in the turret are important in that they allow steam to be cut off outside the cab in the event of a failure of a valve or pipe in the cab, resulting in the cab being filled with steam.

Some locomotives had a slanted front cab wall, as seen in the photo above.

Most locomotives had one or more ventilation hatches in the cab roof. These are clearly visible on C&O 1132 (above) and NKP 175 (below).

Part 6: The Tender

The tender carries the locomotive's fuel and water supply, and being permanently coupled to the locomotive is really part of it.

The tender for C&O 2744 is fairly typical for a large superpower locomotive, carrying 21,000 gallons of water and 30 tons of coal. While not often appreciated, the weight of the water is significant. Since water weighs about 8.3 pounds per gallon, the 21,000 gallons in this tender weigh more than 87 tons, almost 3 times as much as the coal!

This tender on a C&O Allegheny (2-6-6-6) further illustrates the weight of the water – it holds 25 tons of coal and 25,000 gallows (104 tons) of water, and requires an 8 wheel truck at the rear to carry the weight of the water.

This Santa Fe oil tender is similar in capacity, holding 7,000 gallons of fuel oil (at about 8 pounds per gallon, 28 tons) and 24,500 gallons of water (102 tons), and is fitted with two eight wheel trucks.

To hold this weight, modern tenders were constructed with a cast underframe that incorporated the bottom of the water space (hence the name water bottom tender.)

To help control the motion of the water in the tender (would you want 80 tons or so of water sloshing around?), the water tank in a tender is fitted with an extensive set of vertical baffles, as seen in this construction photo.

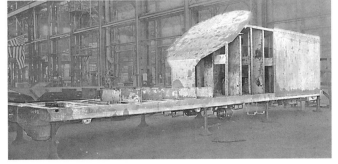

73

There had to be a variety of connections between the tender and the locomotive, including the drawbar(s), which transmit the pulling force of the locomotive to the train, the fuel connection, and the water connections.

Along with the rectangular construction shown here, railroads used the Vanderbilt tender with its cylindrical water tank. For a given water capacity, the cylindrical tank uses less steel than a rectangular tank. But for water capacities above 16,000 gallons or so, either the tank diameter or length became prohibitive, and a rectangular tank had to be used.

Another type of tender that came into common use in the last days of steam was the "centipede" tender, so called because of its multitude of wheels, as shown in this tender for a New York Central Niagara (4-8-4). The complex underframe was a single casting that incorporated the bottom of the water space.

Of course, you had to have a way of putting the fuel and water into the tender, and this was accomplished by loading from the top. The coal bunker was open, to allow easy loading, but the water tank was enclosed and filled through one or more hatches in the tank top, as was the oil bunker on oil burning locomotives.

J. Parker Lamb photo, Thomas W. Dixon Collection

Left Above: Southern Pacific class AC-9 2-8-8-4 #3809 at Kansas City, MO, November, 1939.

Left Below: Lehigh Valley class T-1a 4-8-4 #5106. Note the presence of a booster on the rear tender truck.

Above: N&W class A 2-6-6-4 #1208 departing Columbus, Ohio southbound in September, 1957.

Above: oil burning Southern Pacific class GS-6 4-8-4 #4460

Below: A nice view of the tender of Nickel Plate class S 2-8-4 #706 at Ft. Wayne, Indiana, October, 1936.

Part 7: "Different" Locomotives

By "different" here I mean locomotives that are essentially like the "mainstream" design locomotives that I've described thus far, but different in some particular way.

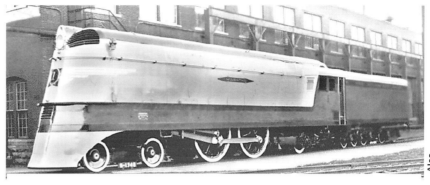

Streamlined Locomotives

Late in the days of steam many railroads streamlined some locomotives used in passenger service. The streamlining was purely cosmetic, as the air resistance of the locomotive is negligible compared to its rolling resistance, and had no effect on the operation of the locomotive, which remained quite conventional in overall design under the shell, even though some appliances were often repositioned from their usual locations to allow for the shroud, as shown here in these illustrations of a Milwaukee Road streamlined Atlantic used in *Hiawatha* service.

In addition to being built new streamlined, many railroads streamlined existing locomotives, like the Frisco locomotive below.

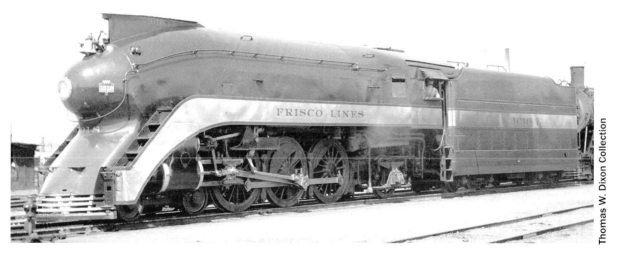

Cab Forward Locomotives

The Southern Pacific railroad, with its many tunnels and snowsheds in the Sierra Nevada mountains, found that engine crewmen were safer and more comfortable if the locomotive were run cab first, putting the cab in front of the exhaust stack. This was possible because these locomotives were oil fired, allowing the fuel for the firebox to be piped forward from the tender. While certainly a success, the SP remained the only railroad to employ locomotives of this type.

Duplex Drive Locomotives

At first glance these locomotives appear to be conventional simple articulateds, but they aren't. There is no hinge in the frame, which is rigid from front to back. The reasoning behind this design is that by splitting the drive over four smaller cylinders, the mass of the pistons and rods was minimized, significantly reducing dynamic augment (see p.44). While several roads experimented with Duplexes (or Duplexi, as they were sometimes called), only the Pennsylvania Railroad placed significant numbers of these unusual beasts into service, fielding 52 of the T1 4-4-4-4s in passenger service and 26 of the Q2 4-4-6-4s freight service.

Bud Laws Collection

PRR class T1 4-4-4-4 (above) and class Q2 4-4-6-4 (below)

Harold K. Vollrath Collection

Water Tube Boilers and High Pressure

A number of railroads and builders experimented with locomotives whose boiler pressure was much higher than usual, on the theory that the higher pressure would result in a more efficient and/or more powerful locomotive. Coupled with the use of a high boiler pressure was compounding, usually in the form of a three or four cylinder compound, and sometimes using triple expansion, where a high pressure cylinder exhausts into a medium pressure cylinder, which in turn exhausts into one or more low pressure cylinders. Generally speaking, none of these experiments worked out, as the higher boiler pressure and complex compound drive resulted in much higher maintenance requirements, effectively negating any savings that would have resulted from the use of the higher efficiency higher capacity locomotive.

Both the Baltimore and Ohio and the Delaware and Hudson railroads were well known for their experiments with high pressure locomotives. Less well known was the New York Central Class HS-1b 4-8-4, which had a boiler pressure of 850 psi, perhaps the highest pressure used on a conventional drive steam locomotive in North America.

NYC HS-1b High Pressure compound 4-8-4

The approach used by George Emerson of the Baltimore and Ohio, incorporating a water-tube firebox with an otherwise conventional boiler, was also used by the Baldwin Locomotive Works on their 350 psi 4-10-2 #60,000, which toured the country in the mid-1920s. Had Lima's super-power designs not appeared, this locomotive might have caught on, since it was fairly successful, and mostly did what Baldwin said it would. However, the relative simplicity of the super-power designs made the complexity of the 60000's boiler and machinery unnecessary.

Baldwin Locomotive Works 4-10-2 #60000. Unlike other three cylinder 4-10-2s, this locomotive was a compound. It used a second Walschaerts valve gear hung on the right side to time the valve for the center cylinder.

*The 60000's boiler, showing the water tube firebox
prominently*

Camelbacks

In the eastern United States, anthracite, or hard coal, was plentiful, and a number of railroads used it as locomotive fuel, particularly in the form of culm, or fines from the mining operation. This fuel burns very slowly compared to other forms of coal and thus requires a very large grate and accompanying firebox. The firebox was so large, in fact, that if the cab was placed in the conventional location engineers had trouble seeing forward around it. Consequently, locomotives were designed to place the cab astride the boiler ahead of the firebox, affording engineers a much better view, but at the expense of separating the engineer and fireman, who had to remain at the back of the locomotive to fire the beast. These locomotives came to be called *camelbacks* or *Mother Hubbards*, and were built into the 1920s, when safety concerns led the Interstate Commerce Commission to forbid any further construction of the type. Existing locomotives were allowed to remain in service though, so camelbacks were common sights on a number of Eastern roads into the 1950s.

Geared Locomotives

These unusual looking locomotives have conventional boilers and cylinders, but rather than being connected to the driving wheels with rods, the cylinders drive a shaft or set of shafts that was then geared to the wheels. The advantages of this arrangement are that is provides smoother torque to the wheels, making these locomotives very sure footed, and that it is very flexible, allowing the locomotive to operate on very rough track. These attributes made these locomotives ideal for logging, mining, and other similar settings.

There are three main types of geared locomotive:

The Shay, with three cylinders driving a drive shaft on the right side of the locomotive that is geared directly to each driving wheel.

Lima

The Climax, with two inclined cylinders, one on each side, driving a cross shaft that in turn drives a longitudinal drive shaft on the center line of the locomotive that is geared to each axle.

Author Photo

The Heisler, with two cylinders in a vee arrangement that drive a longitudinal drive shaft along the locomotive centerline that is geared to the outer axle of each truck. Side rods connect the outer wheels to the inner wheels.

Heisler Locomotive Works Photo

Fireless Locomotives

This is a steam locomotive without a firebox or boiler. The boiler is replaced with a large insulated steam storage tank which contains a charge of steam and hot water. As steam is used, the water boils, creating more steam. Because of their low maintenance requirements these locomotives were popular in industrial settings, and were frequently used in areas where an open flame would be a safety hazard, like a chemical or petroleum plant. Steam is supplied from a stationary boiler on the plant grounds, and a charge can usually last for about 6 - 8 hours.

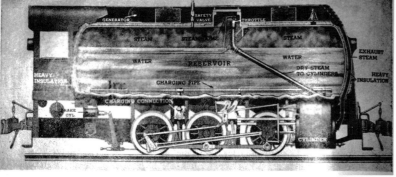

Porter

Above: Delaware and Hudson 0-8-8-0 #1612. Note the massive low pressure cylinders with their slide valves on this Mallet compound locomotive.

Below: Reading class I-9sb 2-8-0 #1633 at St. Clair, Pennsylvania, in October 1948. The Wooten type firebox is extra wide to allow the use of slow burning anthracite coal.

Above: Southern Pacific class AC-4 cab-forward 4-8-8-2 #4102.

Below: The large oil and water tender of SP class AC-8 cab-forward 4-8-8-2 turning on the Cascade Wye. Note the condensation on the sides of the tender, showing the water level inside.

Above: The bullet nose and skyline casing are reminders that Western Pacific 4-8-4 #485 was built to the same plans as Southern Pacific's GS-6 Daylight 4-8-4s. The smoke deflectors, though, are unique to the WP engines.

Below: Pennsylvania Railroad's prototype Q2 #6131 at Altoona Yard in 1944. Note the unusual oblong stack, wider at the rear than the front, because the rear stack is larger than the front one, essentially mirroring the relative dimensions of the front and rear cylinders.

Joe Schmitz Collection

Two Beauties and a Beast

Above: Widely regarded as the most beautiful of streamlined steam locomotives, Southern Pacific class GS-3 4-8-4 #4412 at Los Angeles in 1938 on the inaugural run of the Coast Daylight.

Upper Right: Another highly regarded streamlined steam locomotive, B&O class P-7D streamlined 4-6-2, designed by B&O Research Engineer Olive Dennis. #5303 is at Grafton W.Va. on Aug. 15, 1947.

Lower Right: Streamlined with a less happy result, AT&SF 4-6-4 #3460.

photo by H.N. Barr, Thomas W. Dixon Collection

Joe Schmitz Collection

Above: Southern Pacific GS-4 4-8-4 #4449 at San Francisco, California, July, 1953. Note the side mounted air pumps peaking out from under the skirting above the drivers.

A trio of Pennsylvania streamliners:

Right Above: PRR's first duplex, S1 6-4-4-6 #6100 at Chicago on June 28, 1941, on The General, *its regular assignment.*

Right Below: PRR K4s 4-6-2 #3678 at East St. Louis, Ill.

Below:PRR semi-streamlined K4s 4-6-2 #5338 at E. St. Louis, Missouri in October, 1947, essentially the same as 3678 but without the nose shroud..

Three from the South, one from Up North:
Above: Southern streamlined Ps-4 4-6-2 #1380.
Right Above: N.C.&St.L. (Dixie Lines) 4-8-4 #573.
Right Below: GTW class U-4-b 4-8-4 #6405 at Chicago in June, 1948.
Below: ACL 4-8-4 #1808.

Thomas W. Dixon Collection

A.R. Hoffman Photo, COHS Collection

Above: C&O class L-1 streamlined 4-6-4, equipped with Franklin Type A poppet valves.

Right: C&O class K-4 2-8-4 #2746.

C&O Railway Photo, COHS Collection

Afterword

This book had its genesis in my desire to understand, at a basic level, how a locomotive works. Having been trained in physics, I assumed that the operation of the locomotive and its performance abilities would be able to be understood by the application of basic physical principals, including dynamics, thermodynamics, and the behavior of gasses. As things eventually turned out, I was only partially successful in that effort; the results for the most part are contained in the Technical Details sections of this book, although generally not at quite the level of detail that I have plumbed in my own studies – not everyone has a graduate degree in physics or mechanical engineering, and you shouldn't need them to read a book of this sort. I have to say, though, that I learned a lot in the effort, and thought that others may find what I learned, and my own unique approach to the subject, interesting.

There are a lot of things this book is not, among them a history of steam locomotives, detailed discussions of the locomotives of any particular railroad or builder, or detailed descriptions of the performance of various locomotives. My goal here has been to describe the various parts and basics of design and operation of a modern steam locomotive, as built and used in North America. In the process of writing, I have discovered just how many important parts there are, and how much diversity can occur in the design of those parts.

In writing a book like this, it is difficult to decide what to include and what to omit, particularly when constraints in time and resources are taken into account. I've tried to make a balanced presentation here, covering all the important items without going overboard.

Acknowledgments and References

Writing this book has been, in many ways, like writing a graduate thesis. If that is so, then my thesis advisor has been Bill Withuhn of the Smithsonian Institution. Without his many hours of invaluable discussion on the finer points, this book would have been much less than what it has become.

Almost all of the photographs in this presentation are from the collection of the Chesapeake and Ohio Historical Society, Inc. (COHS) or from the personal collection of Tom Dixon, the society's President Emeritus and Chief Historian . Many of the illustrations are from *Manual for Locomotive Firemen*, published by the C&O Railway for its enginemen, and reprinted by the COHS.

The section on Poppet Valves relies very heavily on two sources: a series of articles by Bill Withuhn published in *The Railroad Enthusiasts Bulletin* in 1975 and 1976, and Franklin Railway Supply Co.Bulletin No. 25, *The Franklin System of Steam Distribution*. Both were provided to me by Tom Dixon.

I'm grateful to all the people who reviewed the manuscript at various stages in its development. They include Bill Withuhn, Tom Dixon, Frank Bongiovanni, Dave Stephenson, Preston Cook, Max Robin, and Phil Shuster. If I've missed anyone, please accept my apologies and thanks.

For those who might be interested in further study, the following books will be helpful:

The Steam Locomotive in America – Its Development in the Twentieth Century, by Alfred W. Bruce.

This is one of the classic books on steam locomotive design, written by the chief engineer of the American Locomotive Company. Rather hard to find now, but worth the search. Bonanza did a lower quality reprint in the 1960s, this edition is still quite adequate, and much cheaper on the used book market.

The Steam Locomotive, by Ralph P. Johnson, M.E.

Another classic on steam locomotive design, by the chief engineer at the Baldwin Locomotive Works. Again, it may be hard to find, but was reprinted not all that long ago. I found my new copy through a mail-order railroadannia catalog.

Locomotive Cyclopedia, 1930, 1938, 1941, 1944, 1947, 1951 editions, if you can find one.

These are a treasure trove of information of steam locomotive design and appliances. Sadly, they are very expensive, even the reprint of the 1941 Edition that was done by Kalmbach publishing 40 years ago.

A Study of the Locomotive Boiler, by Lawford H. Fry

Long out of print, but worth hunting down for its clear explanation of the combustion process and heat transfer properties of a locomotive boiler.

Perfecting the American Steam Locomotive, by J. Parker Lamb

A very well done and readable description of the evolution of locomotive design in North America.

The Steam Locomotive – A Century of North American Classics, by Jim Boyd

One of my favorite "overview" books, this is full of Jim's excellent color photography of preserved (and in most cases operable) steam locomotives.